winning
basketball

Gail Goodrich's
winning basketball

Gail Goodrich with Rich Levin

Contemporary Books, Inc.
Chicago

Thanks to Jim Roark for most of the photographs
in this book and to Del Tanner for valuable
consulting assistance.

Published by Contemporary Books, Inc.
180 North Michigan Avenue, Chicago, Illinois 60601
Manufactured in the United States of America
Library of Congress Catalog Card Number: 78-59058
International Standard Book Number: 0-8092-8108-2 (cloth)
0-8092-8107-4 (paper)

Published simultaneously in Canada by
Beaverbooks
953 Dillingham Road
Pickering, Ontario L1W 1Z7
Canada

contents

As a high school senior in 1961, I was small and skinny, but a determined player.

introduction

My love affair with basketball, which remains intact to this day, began when I was a youngster. It never was a chore, nor was it a sacrifice. Even though I came from an athletic background (my father, Gail, Sr., was an all-Pacific Coast guard at the University of Southern California), I wasn't forced to play. My father introduced me to the sport, as he did to all sports, and he patiently taught me the fundamentals.

While most kids my age were working on their cars or going to the beach or drinking a few beers, I was playing basketball. Many of the other things teen-agers did never appealed to me. Sure, I had friends and I went to the beach now and then, but just standing on street corners hanging out and smoking cigarettes wasn't for me. Instead of the smell of cars, I loved the smell of gyms. I liked the sweat and the feel of the basketball, but most of all I loved the competition.

I wasn't motivated by dreams of future earnings, either. I didn't know a thing about money. Besides, professional basketball players didn't earn much then. Even today, good high school players who spend all day in gyms are not driven by the money they someday may make. They are there because they enjoy the game, and that's the way it should be.

To be proficient, it takes a lot of dedication. You have to master the fundamentals, you have to coordinate your body movement, and you have to develop your shooting. I can't count the hours I spent playing, but I can assure you I spent plenty. In fact, the only times I remember not playing were when I ate or slept. I had a basket rigged to our garage in the backyard and played long after the sun went down. In the house, I would bounce the ball as I went from room to room, twirl it on my finger, and pass it against the walls. It used to drive my mother nuts, but I couldn't help it. I was possessed.

I learned one important lesson: if you're good, boy, you really have fun. It's no fun to go out there and be humiliated. You get depressed and the game loses its attraction. I found if I could play good defense and stop my man from scoring, I would get the ball. Then it was time for offense. And everyone likes to score.

I always tried to play against older, more mature kids, which was difficult to do because I rarely got chosen by them in games. I remember a breakthrough, though, when I was a ninth-grader.

I was 5-foot-1 and weighed 99 pounds at the outside. But I thought I was a fairly good junior high school player. I lived three blocks from the high school and I walked there every day during the Christmas holidays. That was the height of the high school basketball season and everyone had two weeks of vacation, during which basketball was played all day everyday. No games were scheduled and coaches were not permitted to supervise. Consequently, the players worked out on their own and played three-on-three.

Three-on-three half-court basketball is fun and a convenient vehicle for learning practically all aspects of the game. Since fewer players are involved, the court is wide open, giving you more room for movement on offense—which compels you to play better and more tenacious defense.

(Facing page.) Years later as a pro, I'm still relatively small. I'm just as determined and possess a great love for the game.

Being ambitious and somewhat confident, I wanted to play in those games. I would get there at 10 in the morning when the coach opened the gym and would stay until 5 that evening when the coach kicked me out. At first, I just hung around innocuously shooting on the side baskets. I waited and waited and waited, but nobody would choose me. They didn't take me seriously because I was so small. Eventually a few players left; finally I got my chance when one of the remaining players motioned to me and said, "I'll take him." I was the only one left on the sidelines.

What a great experience! I was nervous, but I played well, better than they thought I would. After a few games I reached the point where I was acceptable as a player.

I returned every day. I certainly wasn't the first player picked, nor was I the fourth or fifth, but I was chosen—that was the important thing. At that time, I couldn't shoot from 20 feet, but I had some moves and could drive to the basket. I could pass the ball well and I moved quickly. There was no question that all the others were older, bigger, and better, but I was a feisty competitor who wasn't intimidated.

After the Christmas holidays, the months rolled along; when Easter vacation arrived, I was at the high school again. The season was finished, but all those players who were coming back the next season played. By then, I knew most of the players and I always got to play. I still was a ninth-grader. Although I never realized it at the time, my playing against the high school kids during vacations gave my future coach, Nelson Burton, an opportunity to look me over. In retrospect, his influence turned out to be one of the biggest breaks of my career.

Against better players, you must play better and harder or you won't play. At times, however, you should play against kids your own age and size in order to rekindle your confidence, because there will be days when those bigger youngsters will just destroy you. I always tried to play against better competition. It helped me, and I would encourage all young players to do the same. You will discover that your basketball skills will develop much faster.

The important thing to remember is that a boy, regardless of size, can succeed in a game like basketball (which is dominated by tall boys and men) through dedication, aggressiveness, and perseverance.

winning
basketball

chapter one

fundamentals

The fundamentals are the foundation of basketball. A player cannot be successful unless he successfully masters them. Once he does, he can integrate his mastery into the whole concept of the game.

A basketball doesn't go through the hoop because of pure luck, nor does a pick and roll succeed by accident. Certain maneuvers work because the basic techniques are understood by those involved and executed properly. One shouldn't have to pause during a game to decide what must be done; he should instinctively know. Basketball, a game of habits, should be learned correctly at an early age to preclude the intrusion of bad habits—which become increasingly more difficult to break as one grows older.

To learn the fundamentals and polish his skills, a player must break the game down into such basic phases as body balance and pivoting, ball handling, shooting, rebounding, individual and team defense, and offense. There are drills for each, which must be practiced regularly. Practice never ends for a basketball player; neither does the stress placed on fundamentals.

BODY BALANCE AND PIVOTING

Body balance and pivoting are often overlooked or taken for granted. They are basic to the game and essential in every phase. Body balance is the ability to control the actions of your body and pivoting is an extension of footwork, the foundation of one's balance.

Here are some suggestions to help you achieve proper body balance:

—Have a strong base. In most situations, your feet should be apart, about shoulder-width. If they are too close together, a bump can knock you off balance; if they are too far apart, you won't be ready to move quickly.

—Weight is evenly distributed on the balls of your feet.

—Your head and chin are up so you can make maximum use of your peripheral vision. Be alert. You want to see the entire court.

—Keep your hands close to your body in the area of your chest. Your fingers are spread and relaxed. Be ready to move quickly.

—Your knees are bent. Height is important in basketball, but it is useless if your knees are locked; it will prevent you from moving with quickness.

—Be relaxed. You can't move quickly when you are tense.

Practically all moves in basketball require a pivot. You frequently pivot before taking a shot; and you may pivot while dribbling, rebounding, and defending. Pivoting eventually should become a reflex action. There are two basic pivots, the front and reverse, and the same principles are involved in each.

The basic difference between the two is that the player swings his body towards the defender for the front pivot and swings it away for

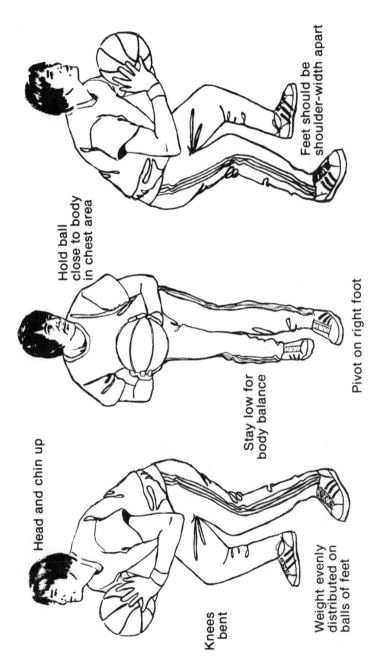

Hold ball close to body in chest area

Feet should be shoulder-width apart

Stay low for body balance

Pivot on right foot

REVERSE PIVOT

Head and chin up

Knees bent

Weight evenly distributed on balls of feet

3

the reverse. When I teach pivoting to boys, I stress the latter because it provides more protection of the ball.

Here's how pivoting is executed:

—Moving at full speed, pull up, landing on both feet simultaneously, with your head up, arms close to your body, tail low, and knees bent. If you land on both feet, you have the option of using either foot as your pivot foot.

—Your feet should be approximately shoulder-width apart when you land.

—If you have the ball, protect it with a firm grip close to your body above your waist.

—If you're making a right-foot pivot, pick up your left foot, turn on the ball of your right foot, swing your left around 180 degrees, and put your left foot down.

—To make a left-foot pivot, pick up your right foot and swing to your left.

BALL HANDLING

Every basketball player must handle the ball. You must be able to dribble, pass, and receive. You are crippled offensively if you can't. All good teams have five men who can adequately move the ball up and down the court.

Some tips for handling the ball include the following:

—Whether shooting, dribbling, passing, or receiving, control the ball with your fingertips.

—Always protect the ball. Keep it close to your body.

—Whenever you move the ball, move it quickly.

—Keep your head up at all times. Good vision is important.

Passing

All good teams can pass the ball quickly and accurately. It is the best way to move the ball. The defense finds it difficult to react to good passing teams. The teammate who works hard to get open for a shot expects to receive the ball. If you can hit the open man, you will be a tremendous asset to your team.

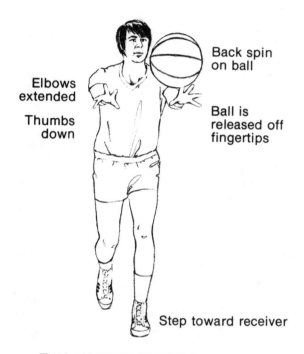

Back spin
on ball

Elbows
extended

Thumbs
down

Ball is
released off
fingertips

Step toward receiver

TWO-HANDED CHEST PASS

With the defensive player applying pressure on you, it becomes necessary to pass over and around him. Therefore, you should know how to use the various kinds of passes: the one- and two-handed chest pass, the one- and two-handed bounce pass, the overhead pass, the baseball pass, the handoff, and the hook pass.

The two-handed chest pass is used to get the ball to a teammate quickly. Usually there won't be a defender between you and the receiver. The same principles apply for the one-handed chest pass, which I find effective to throw off the dribble on the fast break.

—Make the pass crisply, but not too hard.
—Your target is the receiver's mid-chest area.
—Take a step to your receiver when making the pass to maintain body balance.

In a game situation, I'm about to use the overhead pass to get the ball into the pivot. Notice that the pass will go over Dick Van Arsdale's right shoulder, not to his left where his arm is raised to deflect the pass.

—Make the pass with reverse spin to make it easier for the receiver to handle the ball.

—Snap the pass off the fingertips with elbows extended and thumbs down.

The bounce pass, which also can be thrown either one- or two-handed, is effective when there is a defender between the passer and receiver. It's a pass that should be used in heavy traffic because it is much more difficult to pick off or deflect than the chest pass. Use it on the fast break to cover short distances. If thrown properly, it is easy to handle.

—Push the bounce pass off the fingertips.

Hold ball high
above head—
release with a
flick of the wrists

OVERHEAD PASS

—It should bounce approximately two-thirds of the way from passer to receiver.

—Put reverse spin on the pass to make it easier for the receiver to handle.

—The ball should be received about waist-high. Otherwise it will be difficult for your teammate to receive the ball on the run.

The overhead pass is a two-handed pass thrown over a guarding defensive player. It is a short pass, often used to feed the center.

—The ball is held high, directly over the head, and is released with a flicking of the wrists to the receiver.

—Pass it quickly but not too hard.

—Hit the target that the receiver or center will provide away from the defender.

The baseball pass travels a long distance in a hurry and is a particularly effective outlet pass to start the fast break. This pass should be thrown to a receiver who is wide open; it is not advisable to throw the pass in heavy traffic.

—Take a step forward and snap your wrist toward the receiver. It is thrown much like a catcher's throw to second base.
—This is a difficult pass to control, and accuracy is important. A careless passer may hook the ball, creating a turnover.
—Make the pass quickly. Don't spend much time winding up. The longer it takes you to wind up, the more chance the defense has to recover and possibly intercept the ball.

The handoff is used to get the ball to a teammate cutting off you. You will find it effective while working a two-on-two situation or a weave.

—Use your body to protect the ball. Stand between the defender and the ball. Be in a crouch position with knees bent, head up. Maintain good body balance.
—Hold the ball waist-high with your palm up.
—When your teammate cuts past, give the ball a little flick upwards so it pops out of your hand. Make sure it doesn't pop too high, as it will be difficult for your teammate to control.

The hook pass is vital when you are heavily guarded and forced to turn your back on the play. The passer takes one step to the side and hooks the ball around the defender. You often will see this pass used to feed the pivot.

No matter what kind of pass you use, there are several general pointers that should be observed:

—Pass the ball quickly. It should be crisp, but not too hard.
—Keep your head up to maintain maximum vision. You must be aware of where the defensive players are as well as your teammates.

Snap wrist—ball
is released off
fingertips

Shift weight to front
foot as you step forward
toward receiver

BASEBALL PASS

—Release the ball with backspin.

—Make sure the pass can be received in the area of the waist and chest.

—Don't telegraph the pass. Learn to fake your passes.

—Make the pass accurate. Careless passing creates turnovers.

—After making the pass, be ready to move quickly. Don't stand around.

Receiving the ball is a continuation of the pass. The receiver's primary job is simply to catch the ball.

Important reminders are:

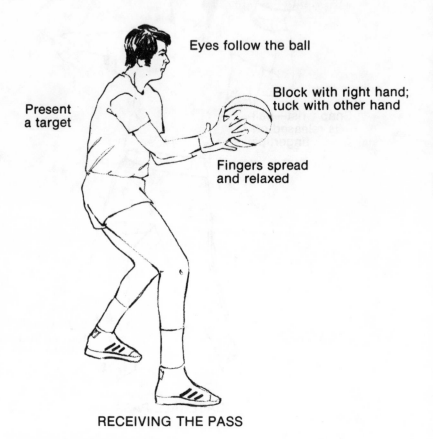

Eyes follow the ball

Block with right hand;
tuck with other hand

Present
a target

Fingers spread
and relaxed

RECEIVING THE PASS

—Work hard to get open. The more open you are, the more often you will get the ball.

—Be ready to receive the pass at any time.

—Present a target away from the defender if possible.

—Fingers are spread and relaxed.

—Eyes follow the flight of the ball until it is caught.

—Block the ball with one hand and tuck with the other.

—Make a quick move after receiving the ball. Don't hold it.

Dribbling

Dribbling is an offensive tool that allows an individual to move with

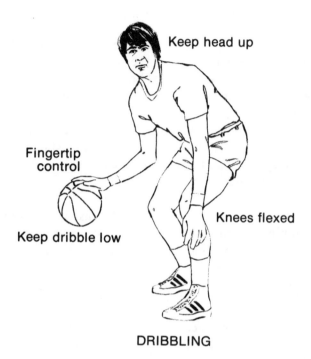

Keep head up

Fingertip control

Knees flexed

Keep dribble low

DRIBBLING

the ball from one area of the court to another by himself. It is especially effective for penetrating the defense for a high-percentage shot or creating a play for a teammate.

To become a skilled dribbler requires a great deal of practice and concentration. It is particularly important to be able to dribble well with either hand. Never waste a dribble and always dribble with a purpose. However, don't fall into the habit of dribbling too much.

There are two kinds of dribbling: the control dribble and the speed dribble. The former is used in an offensive setup situation, where it is imperative that the dribbler protect the ball.

Here are some tips to help you with your control dribble:

—Use fingertip control. Your palm may touch the ball, but the control is in the fingertips.

—Wrist is flicked downwards to push the ball.

—Knees are flexed and back is straight. You're in a crouch position.

—Protect the ball by keeping it close to your body. Your body is between the defender and the ball.

—Keep the dribble low. It should bounce no higher than the knee. The lower you can dribble, the more difficult it is for the defender to flick away.

—Don't watch the ball while dribbling. An accomplished dribbler will have the ball under control. You must have good vision. It is very important to see how the defense is set up and where your teammates are.

The speed dribble usually is used on the fast break when the dribbler is running at full speed. The quickest way to get the ball upcourt is to pass; the next quickest way is to use the speed dribble. A few reminders are:

—Push the ball out in front of you.

—Run to meet the ball.

—The dribble will bounce higher than it will for the controlled dribble; usually it will bounce waist-high.

SHOOTING

All basketball players must score. It is basic to the game. To be an offensive threat, you must have the capability of making a variety of shots from different positions on the floor.

Good shooters are very confident. They believe every shot they take will go in. You may miss five straight, but you must believe the next five will fall. Some will be missed, but you will find the good shooters shoot better than 45 percent.

Shooting is one phase of the game you can practice by yourself. All you need is a hoop and a basketball. When you work on your shots, pay particular attention to the ones you expect to take in the

Dribbling against Dick Snyder of the Cleveland Cavaliers, my head is up for good vision and my body is balanced. My right arm is raised slightly to protect the ball. Snyder is in good defensive position, being ahead of the dribbler to prevent the drive.

My good friend and teammate, Pat Riley, shows good form on this shot. His right elbow is under the ball, the ball is being released off the fingertips and directly above the head, his left hand and arm (which act as a guide) are coming off the ball, and his eyes are focused on the rim.

game. You are wasting time by just practicing low-percentage and off-balance shots. If possible, simulate game conditions by going one-on-one with a friend. You can also use your imagination by devising shooting games.

Everyone shoots differently and everyone has his own style. Develop a shot you find comfortable. The results are far more important than the looks, but there are basic fundamentals that should be observed to make you a high-percentage shooter.

—A shooter must have good body balance. Many shots are released while the shooter is in the air, making body control important. The shoulders should be squared off and facing the basket, the feet shoulder-width apart, and the weight evenly distributed.

—Your knees are bent for balance and body control as you prepare to take the shot.

—Keep the ball close to your body, about chest-high, before taking the shot. Hold the ball tightly, but not too firmly, with your fingers and the upper portion of your hand.

—Keep the elbow of your shooting arm close to your body and directly under the ball.

—Your nonshooting hand acts as a guide and is released just before you shoot.

—Release the ball off your fingertips to give you a slow reverse spin for the desired soft touch.

—As you release the ball, reach out to the basket and follow through with your elbow and arm fully extended.

—Focus your eyes on either the front or back rim. I recommend the latter because a tired player doesn't jump as high and tends to shoot short. Shooting for the back rim gives the shooter a greater margin for error. However, some great shooters concentrate on the front rim, so each player must make his own decision on where to aim.

—On close-in shots, you may use the backboard. Pick out a particular spot on the backboard where the ball will hit and carom into the basket.

—Shoot with an arc that you find comfortable. Much will depend upon where you release the ball. But it is desirable to

have a natural medium arc—not too high and not too flat.
   —Shoot the ball quickly, but don't hurry.
   —After the shot, immediately get back into the play. Be prepared to rebound or to fall back on defense.

There are a variety of shots players can take, some of which are

Release ball off
fingertips at
peak of jump

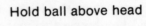
Hold ball above head

Non-shooting hand
on side of ball
acts as guide

Keep elbow
directly
under ball

Focus eyes on rim

Shoulders face
squarely toward
basket

Jump straight up

JUMP SHOT

Taking a jump shot against the taller Oscar Robertson, I release the ball at the peak of my jump. However, I'm fading away from the basket, which can reduce the chances of making the shot.

created on the spot or dictated by the defense. But the most frequently used are the jump shot, the driving layin, and the free throw.

Jump Shot

The jump shot is the most popular and effective shot in the game today. A good jump shooter can hit consistently from a range of 20 feet. The shooter has a great advantage if he can turn quickly and shoot off the dribble. To do so, he must stop and pivot for good body balance. How quickly the shooter stops and releases the ball is more important than how high he jumps.

Here are some pointers for shooting the jump shot:

—When moving to your right, stop on your left foot (the foot closest to the basket) and pivot by bringing the right foot around so your body is squared off facing the basket. Then go up for the shot. When moving to the left, do the opposite.

—Jump straight up and come straight down. Don't fall away. Falling away makes the shot more difficult and will lower your shooting percentage.

—Release the ball at the peak of your jump.

—Keep the ball in front of you above your head. It should not be too far back behind your head. In that position there is a tendency to throw the ball rather than shoot it. How high a player holds the ball above his head varies with individual style.

Layin

As far as I'm concerned, there are two kinds of layins—what I call the baby or short hook and the regular layin. The baby hook is used by many players to elude taller defenders on the way to the basket. I find this an easy way to shoot many of my driving layins.

—Hold the ball away from the defender with one hand and release it so it hits high on the backboard.

—Bank the ball off the board with a soft touch for better accuracy.

—The nonshooting hand is raised to protect the shot.

—Jump high to the basket like a high jumper. Don't broad-jump.

—Keep your eyes on the target—a spot on the board from where the ball will carom into the basket. Use the painted square on the backboard, if available, as a guide.

—Learn to shoot the layin both right- and left-handed.

The regular layin is often used off the fast break or when the shooter isn't threatened by a defender. A player should be able to

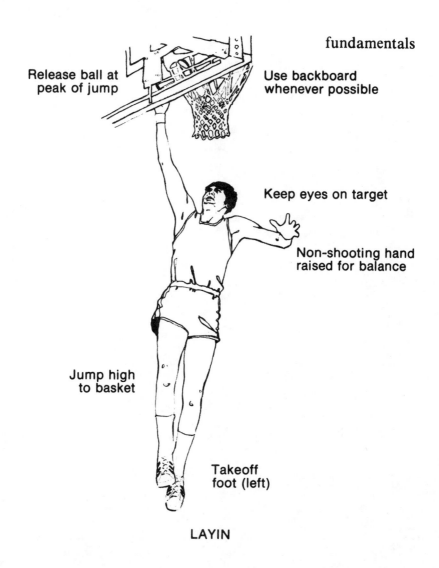

Release ball at peak of jump

Use backboard whenever possible

Keep eyes on target

Non-shooting hand raised for balance

Jump high to basket

Takeoff foot (left)

LAYIN

make this shot with either hand while running at full speed. It should never be missed.

—Release the ball at the peak of your jump with a flip of the wrist. Your palm should be under the ball facing upward to the basket. A younger player, who finds it difficult to shoot with his hand under the ball, might prefer to shoot the layin as he would a push shot.

19

—Normally the shot will be banked off the board from one side or the other. Use the board when possible. Going over the rim is a more difficult shot and sometimes can cause a careless miss.

Free Throw

Free throws play an important part in every game. They are high-percentage shots and good free-throw shooters make 80 percent or more from the line. How many times have you seen games decided at the free-throw line? Include free-throw shooting in every workout, even if you're only shooting around.

There are many different ways to shoot free throws. I have found it best for me to shoot them as I do my jump shots. The only difference is that I don't jump, but I do rise on my toes.

Concentration and rhythm are the most important factors. Most players will go through a ritual when they step to the line. When the official hands me the ball, I bounce it three times to relax and to give me time to concentrate. Then I take aim at a spot on the middle of the back part of the rim and shoot. As with all shots, I am comfortable and relaxed. Remember, the beginning of the shot until the end is one continuous flow of motion.

REBOUNDING

Rebounding is one of the keys in every game. Usually more shots are missed than made during the course of a game; thus the team that controls the board usually will win. If you can get your share or more of the rebounds, you can initiate the fast break and ultimately control the tempo of the game. It will also give you more shots at your end of the floor.

Rebounding is an area of the game in which a player's attitude and aggressiveness pay off. When the rebound comes off the board it is a

(Facing page.) I'm driving hard to the basket, taking the baby hook over defender Dave DeBusschere, formerly of the New York Knicks. The ball is released high and away from the defender and my eyes are focused on the backboard—which I will use to make the shot.

Jump aggressively to the ball

Grab ball high in the air with elbows extended and hands high above the head

Player has completed pivot, so he is now between his man and the basket. Note how he has taken up the space between them

Arms raised; body low for balance and in preparation for jumping

Player in defensive position knows where his man is at all times

REBOUNDING—BOXING OUT

free ball and in many cases it will go to the player who wants it the most.

There are two theories of defensive rebounding. In the first, the rebounder, using his inside position, blocks the offensive man away from the board with a reverse or front pivot. Accordingly, if all five offensive rebounders are properly blocked out, the ball can bounce into the hands of one of the defensive rebounders. In the second theory, the defensive players with inside position merely release to get the ball off the boards.

The latter usually can be accomplished by the few big centers and big jumpers who are situated under the basket or who have exceptional jumping ability. Most players will first block their man out and then release to get the rebound.

For defensive rebounding, I have found the following points to be important:

—Always assume the shot taken will be missed.

—Block your man off the boards using either a front or reverse pivot. Then release quickly and aggressively and go after the ball.

—Arms are up and fingers pointed to the ceiling.

—When you get into position, step into your man, taking up the distance between the two of you. Don't leave him any room to maneuver. If you give your man a step or two, it will give him momentum and he may be able to bump you and knock you off balance.

—Be aggressive and grab the ball with both hands when going for the rebound.

—Bring the ball into your chest and keep your elbows out when coming down with the ball. Don't swing your elbows. If you make contact, you will draw a foul.

—Spread out with your legs and keep your knees bent for good body balance.

—Immediately initiate the outlet pass and be ready to get down the court quickly.

Offensive rebounding is important because you can get the ball

Paul Silas of the Boston Celtics, the NBA's premier rebounding forward, battles my teammate Corky Calhoun (left) and another Laker (behind Silas) for ball.

under or near the basket with the defense out of position. Chances are you will get a good shot or be fouled. Second and third shots can be devastating to the opponent.

Many of the same principles that apply for defensive rebounding also apply for offensive rebounding. Some tips are:

—Be active. The more movement you have, the better the chance of opening rebounding lanes. It also makes it more difficult for the defensive rebounder to block you out.

—Try to anticipate the direction in which the rebound will go. Watch the flight of the shot. You should be able to determine if the shot is long or short. As a player gains experience, he'll get an idea of how the ball comes off the backboard and rim.

—If possible, force the defensive man directly under the basket. The farther under the basket he is, the less chance he will have of getting the rebound. Most balls will bounce a few feet off the rim.

—Always try to get a hand on the rebound. If all you can do is bat it back on the backboard, do it, because you will keep the ball alive. By doing so, you or a teammate may ultimately get the rebound.

—Don't foul unnecessarily. Usually the defensive man will have position. If you go over his back, the referee will call the foul.

DEFENSE

While it is important to put points on the scoreboard, it is just as important to stop the opposition from scoring. All good teams put as much stress on defense as they do on offense. If you play good defense, you can create a turnover or a missed shot, which can trigger your fast break.

Defense essentially is a matter of guarding your man, and you must begin each game believing you will stop him from scoring. It is a challenge you must accept in basketball. So much of defense depends upon one's attitude. Consequently, anybody can become a good defensive player if he puts his mind to it.

As a defender, you first must realize you have an inherent disadvantage. The offensive player has many options, and he knows what he is going to do. The defender doesn't. The defensive player's primary tasks are to eliminate some of those options and to force the offensive player into positions in which he doesn't want to be. The advantage then will shift to the defense.

The basic rule is to stay between your man and the basket. Oftentimes, however, you will want to play the passing lane between your man and the ball, making it difficult for him to receive the pass. You can't prevent him from getting the ball all the time, but if you are aggressive, you sometimes can force him out farther from the basket than he would like to be. Most players like to receive the ball in an operating zone of 15 to 20 feet from the basket. There, good offensive players are hard to stop and the pressure is shifted to the defender. You want the pressure on him, so force him out as far as you can.

Here are some suggestions to help you play better defense:

—Know your opponent's offensive strengths and weaknesses.

—In a defensive position, your knees are bent, you are down low, your feet are spread apart slightly more than the width of your shoulders, your back is straight, and your head and chin are up. Play defense on the balls of your feet.

—Slide your feet when you're moving with your man. Never cross over your feet.

—Know where your man is at all times. In most situations, try to stay within an arm's reach of him. You should be able to reach out and touch his chest. There will be times, however, when you can't. In a spread-court situation or on the run, you will be farther away. When he has the ball, stay close enough to stop the jump shot. But you must still be able to stay with him on the drive.

—Look at your man's midsection while guarding him. He can fake you with his head, his shoulders, and his legs, but he can't go anywhere without his midsection.

—Try to keep ahead of the dribbler. If he's dribbling to the

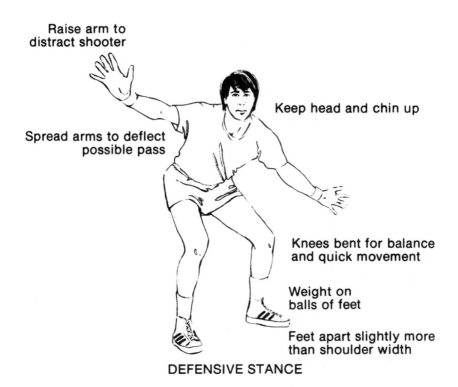

Raise arm to distract shooter

Keep head and chin up

Spread arms to deflect possible pass

Knees bent for balance and quick movement

Weight on balls of feet

Feet apart slightly more than shoulder width

DEFENSIVE STANCE

right, stay a step ahead so he can't put on a burst of speed and go by you.

—When your man is in shooting range, put a hand up in his face to distract the shot. If you're farther out, both hands should be low or to the side to reach for the dribble or to deflect the pass.

—Against the shooter, go straight up and don't reach in. Wave a hand in his eyes to distract him. Make it tough for him to score, but don't put him on the foul line, especially if he is taking a long outside jump shot.

—If you can, put a hand on your man now and then to bother him. Try to upset him as often as you can. Many offensive players don't like contact; they don't like a hand on them, and that's

Stay one arm's length away, lightly touching dribbler's hip to distract him

Keep a step ahead of dribbler to guard against drive

Slide feet

DEFENDING THE DRIBBLER

precisely why you do it. Try to do whatever you can to disrupt his rhythm. If touching and bumping him occasionally will do the trick, then do it. There are limits imposed on contact at each level of the game. You must know the limits the officials will allow.

—When going for a steal, reach in with the inside hand and flip the ball out in front of you. You must be quick. Don't reach with the outside hand because usually you will draw a foul. Remember that defense is played primarily with your feet, not with your hands.

—Try not to foul. It hinders your play and can hurt the chances of your team.

Guarding your man when he doesn't have the ball is the most difficult time to check him. Most of the time he won't have it. Theoretically, each man will have it only one-fifth of the time on offense. It is

Chris Ford of Detroit takes an outside jump shot. I try to distract his shot by jumping straight up with arm outstretched. The chance of blocking an outside shot is slim, so I'm careful not to foul him.

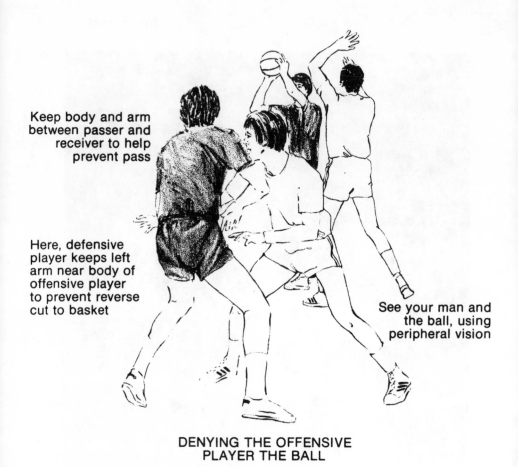

Keep body and arm between passer and receiver to help prevent pass

Here, defensive player keeps left arm near body of offensive player to prevent reverse cut to basket

See your man and the ball, using peripheral vision

DENYING THE OFFENSIVE PLAYER THE BALL

harder for a defender because the offensive player can move much quicker without the ball. Many defenders—not the good ones—tend to relax when the ball is away from their man, figuring he can't score without the ball. But a good defender will make sure his man doesn't get the ball in scoring position.

Some points to consider when guarding your man away from the ball:

—Keep your balance, stay low, and be alert.
—Vision is very important at all times. Be in a position where you can see your man and the ball at the same time.

30

—Play the passing lane between the ball and the offensive player.

Although you will always have a one-on-one responsibility in a man-to-man defense, you must also be conscious of playing defense within the framework of your team. As a team, you're trying to move the offense as far away from the basket as possible. The defense should try to control the tempo of the game and dictate to the offense what it can and cannot run. As a defender, you want to be the aggressor.

Be aware of the entire offense and what it is trying to accomplish—not just your man. You may have to shade your man in a particular direction or perhaps force him into an area where you will get help from your teammates. Your man may have a weakness driving to his left, but you may be required to shade him to his strength because of your team's overall defensive strategy.

While trying to control the tempo of the game, apply pressure to your man as soon as you can. The purpose of pressure is to disrupt the continuity of the offense as well as to control the tempo of the game. If you have a quick, fast team, you can take advantage of those attributes by using pressure. Pick your man up at full or three-quarter court. Where you pick him up normally will depend upon your team's defensive strategy, but there is no reason for allowing him to come up court 47 feet before guarding him. A player doesn't necessarily apply full-court pressure to steal the ball. You do it to let the opponent know the defense is around. Let them know they have to work to get the ball up court. You are giving in to the offense if you allow it to come up court unmolested.

Additional things to remember are:

—Talk to your teammates on defense. The offense will use a lot of picks, so call out what it is doing as a warning to your teammates. Say things like, "Step out . . . Pick left . . . Watch the backdoor. . . ."

—Play the passing angles or passing lanes. There are only so many places the ball can be passed. Be aware of them.

—Be prepared to help your teammates whenever and wherever you can.

31

The Zone

In a zone, your defensive assignment is an area of the court rather than an offensive player. Basically, the defense plays its big men under the basket and its smaller men up front, giving the team a convenient setup for rebounding and the fast break.

The zone stresses the importance of players helping out more than a man-to-man does. It allows more gambling, because the defense can be shifted quickly to cover a man temporarily out of position. It also is valuable when your team has one or two weak defenders, for it can cover up some deficiencies.

However, I don't advocate the use of a zone. The biggest disadvantage is a lack of pressure. The offense can set up unmolested, giving it an edge because it can initiate the play easily. Although the offense may have difficulty penetrating, it has considerable time to work the ball for a high-percentage shot. The zone also is vulnerable to a good offensive rebounding team, because the penetration of the offense in the rebounding lanes is difficult to check. It also can cause a player to pick up bad defensive habits, such as reaching and gambling too much. It is important for all players, particularly young ones, to have sound individual defensive fundamentals. If a player always plays a zone, he may never fully learn the basic principles of playing individual defense, whereas a good individual defensive player can always adjust his game and play a zone.

At times, however, I believe there are zone principles that can be applied to a man-to-man defense. One example is sagging from the weak side and clogging up the middle. Another is the trap in the corner, where the ball can be two-timed. In those instances, you're still in a man-to-man, but you are using some zone principles.

OFFENSE

Offensive basketball is a five-man effort integrating the basic skills of each individual as they pass, dribble, shoot, and rebound. However, there is more to it than that. Since only one player can handle the ball at a time, the other four must learn to move without the ball.

Playing without the ball is an important part of the game, which

THE MOST COMMONLY USED
ZONE DEFENSES

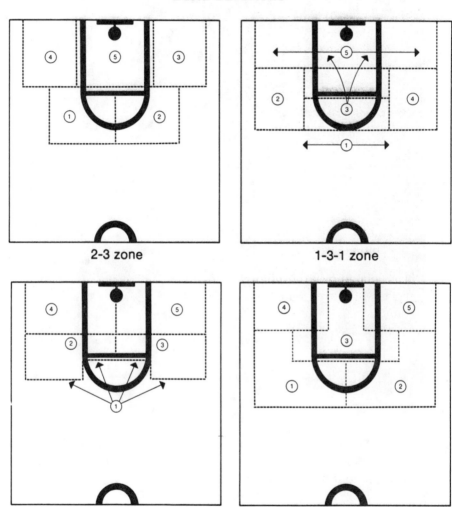

2-3 zone

1-3-1 zone

1-2-2 zone

2-1-2 zone

The diagrams above are intended to show only the initial setup and the areas of responsibility for zone defenses. Of course, the offensive setup and the movement of the ball will affect the defensive players' movement.

Playing without the ball is my forte. Here, I cut by Kareem Abdul-Jabbar and don't get the ball immediately (above) . . .

requires a lot of hard work to master. Some players tend to stand around and watch while others handle the ball. They figure they'll move when the ball reaches them. You should be moving all the time, however. You can make your offensive effort much easier by

I continue cutting to the basket and receive a return pass over the head of defender Brian Winters, who is a step behind me.

setting up your defensive man and by being in position to score when you receive the ball.

There are many things you can do without the ball. Besides setting your man up for an easy score, you can set screens for your teammates, get in rebounding position, or clear through to the weak side to give a teammate room in which to operate.

Here are some suggestions for playing without the ball and setting up your man for the score:

—Most important, constantly be in motion. But there must be a purpose to your movement. Be aware of your plays and where the ball and your defensive man are at all times.

—Coordinate your movements with those of your teammates. The more you help one another, the easier it will be to lose your defender.

—Know how your defensive man plays you without the ball. Will he let you roam freely? Will he bump you? Is he shading you? Is he forcing you out? You must know what he's trying to do so you can set him up.

—Make your movements quickly and take advantage of the edge you have as an offensive player. You know what you want to do; he doesn't.

—Try to get the ball in an area where you can be effective offensively. If you get the ball outside of your operating zone (the area in which you are capable of scoring), you have worked for nothing.

—Once you have set your man up and received the ball inside your operating zone, make your move—a jump shot or a drive—quickly.

One-on-One Moves

Every player must have the capability of beating his defensive man in a one-on-one situation. Keep in mind, however, that your move should be consistent with your team's offensive patterns. With your dribble remaining, the two basic one-on-one moves that can be used to set up the jump shot or the drive are the crossover step and the rocker step.

The crossover step is effective in getting your man moving horizontally, from side to side. Basically, you fake in one direction and go in the other.

Here, player fakes to right by taking a short jab step

Face basket when receiving ball

Hold ball close to body

Cross over with a long right stride to drive left around defensive player

Keep dribble low, out in front, and away from defensive player

CROSSOVER STEP

ROCKER STEP

Fake drive with short jab step to right—weight on front foot.

Rock back on right foot while faking shot with head and ball, thus bringing defensive player up close to defend shot.

On the rocker step, you try to get your man moving vertically, up and back. You fake the drive, come back to fake the jump shot, and go to the basket.

Here are a few important hints for executing the crossover step and the rocker step:

—Keep your balance. Keep your head up so you can see the entire court.

—Face the basket before making your move and hold the ball firmly around the letters.

—When you fake the drive, take a quick, short step and transfer your weight to your front foot.

—If you fake and return to your original position, make sure you are in balance before you take the shot.

Take long stride with right foot around defensive player, accelerating to basket.

—Once you decide to drive, make that first step a long stride to get by the defender. Drive hard and fast to the basket.

—Don't hold the ball too long before making your move. If you do, the defense will have time to adjust.

—Read your defensive man immediately. Is he shading you to one side? Is he guarding against the drive? You have the advantage; use it.

—Be a threat to drive in either direction.

—Mix up your offense to keep the defensive man off balance. You can use a combination of crossover and rocker steps. The possibilities are unlimited.

The good offensive player can also shake a defender with the dribble. To do so he can utilize the following moves: the head and

HEAD AND SHOULDER FAKE WITH DRIBBLE

Dribble straight toward defender
and slow down as you prepare to . . .

shoulder fake, the spin or reverse dribble, the crossover dribble, and
the hesitation or stutter step.

The head and shoulder fake is used to deceive the defensive man.
The dribbler steps and leans with his head and shoulders in one
direction, trying to force the defender off balance, while keeping his
dribble and going the same way.

The spin or reverse dribble is a move used to change direction.
The real advantage in using this move is that the ball is protected at
all times. If the dribbler is moving to his right and dribbling with his
right hand, he stops and makes a reverse pivot on his left foot while
keeping his dribble. He brings the ball across his body, picks up the
next dribble with his left hand, and completes the change of direction. The spin dribble should be used when the defensive man is
applying pressure.

shift all weight to left side of
body while maintaining dribble—

then accelerate past defender to right.

The crossover dribble is a move to beat your man to the basket. The dribbler approaches the defender, pushes the ball quickly across his body, picks up the dribble with his other hand, and continues the drive. The dribbler maintains a good field of vision because he doesn't have to turn his back on his defensive man.

The hesitation or stutter step is a change of pace move. As the dribbler dribbles at full speed, he hesitates for a second as if to stop. When the defensive man relaxes, the dribbler goes by him with a quick burst of speed.

Here are some important reminders for your moves with the dribble:

—Keep your head up. A full field of vision is required to know where the defense is and to be able to hit the open man with a pass in case you are double-teamed.

—Make your move quickly so the weak-side defense can't help out.

—Keep your dribble low and protect the ball.

Two-on-Two Offense

Offensive patterns are designed to create high-percentage shots for good shooters. There are many plays and patterns a coach can implement; most will use cuts and screens to spring a man open. Some will be designed to create a one-on-one situation, but most will require at least a second man. While excellent players can score one-on-one, I find it much easier if I get a screen from my teammate.

Since there are many options in a pattern, timing and execution are important. You must know and understand your role within the play. While we won't discuss the different kinds of patterns here, we will examine the screen and roll, which is the basic two-on-two situation. This play should be learned early in one's career. There are three ways the screen and roll is initiated:

—The dribbler can dribble off the man setting the screen.

—The dribbler can pass to the screener and cut him off without the ball. I find this particularly effective, because you can move and change directions quicker without the ball.

—The dribbler can pass to a receiver, follow the ball, and set a screen for the receiver.

Here's how the screen and roll works:

—The screener establishes position within shooting range—approximately 20 feet from the basket. He spreads out, taking up as much room as possible, and maintains good body balance.

—The dribbler drives by the screener on his way to the basket, forcing his defender to run into the screen.

—When the screener feels contact from the defender, he pivots away from the defender and rolls to the basket.

—The dribbler now has several options: (1) He can continue his drive to the basket. (2) He can stop and take the jump shot. (3) If the defense picks him up, he can pass to the screener, who is breaking to the basket. The bounce pass probably is the best pass to use at this time.

Other effective options in two-on-two situations are the give and go and the backdoor play.

On the give and go, the ball handler will pass the ball to a teammate. If the defender expects the passer to follow the ball, he will overplay him and prevent him from following. The passer then can fake and cut directly to the basket for a return pass. It also can be executed when the defender relaxes after the offensive player passes to a teammate. The passer then should quickly cut to the basket.

The backdoor play is created when the defense overplays an offensive receiver to such an extent that he is denying the pass. When this happens the offensive player should fake to meet the pass and cut to the basket. The passer, meanwhile, will fake the initial pass to the receiver to help draw the defensive man out of position and then will hit his teammate cutting to the basket.

Fast Break

Just about all good professional teams run the fast break. Over the years, the Boston Celtics have had a great fast break and the last two

SCREEN AND ROLL

Offensive player (1) looks
away from screener (3), thus
setting opponent up
for the screen

1

2

3

4

Screener spreads out
and keeps low for balance

Screener (3) establishes
position; offensive player
prepares to dribble off screen

Offensive player (1) dribbles off screener forcing defender (2) into screen

Defensive player (4) steps out, blocking path to basket and/or taking away jump shot from offensive player (1). When screener (3) feels contact from defensive player (2), he does a reverse pivot and cuts to basket. Offensive player (1) throws a bounce pass to screener, who is rolling to the basket.

45

The layin often is the result of a well-executed fast break. By filling the lane, I received the pass for this layin. Rudy Tomjanovich of the Houston Rockets tries to defend.

seasons the Golden State Warriors had much success running. Championship teams possess many characteristics and a well-executed fast break usually is one of them. It is the best offensive weapon a team can possess. To execute it properly, your team must have quickness and good ball-handling skills, which makes it important to have five men capable of running and also handling the ball.

The object of the fast break is to get down court and get a high-percentage shot before the defense has an opportunity to set up.

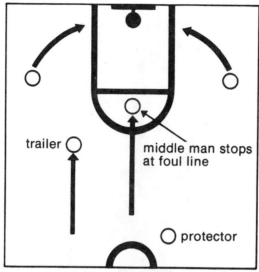

trailer

middle man stops
at foul line

protector

FINISH OF THE FAST BREAK

Since the court is spread on the fast break, you don't have to contend with a pressure defense and consequently your shooting percentage will be higher.

Some principles for effectively executing the fast break are:

—Get the defensive rebound. You can't run without the ball.

—Make the outlet pass quickly and make it to a guard.

—Get the ball in the middle of the court as soon as possible.

—Pass the ball down court with as little dribbling as possible. You want to get down court quickly and the fastest way is to pass.

—Fill the lanes. A balanced fast break should have the dribbler in the middle, a man on each of the wings, and a trailer. This enables the middle man the option of passing to either side, going all the way, stopping and taking the jump shot, or waiting and hitting the trailer.

—The trailer is important. The defense may stop the initial fast break, but the trailer gives your break an odds-on situation, like a 4-on-3 advantage.

chapter two

the game

When James Naismith invented basketball 84 years ago at a Springfield, Massachusetts, YMCA, he could not foresee the evolution of the game. He could not imagine the jump shot, the fast break, the zone press, or the "sky hook." He could not picture his game being pumped into homes across America via television and he could not sympathize with the millions of youngsters who would spend hour upon hour toiling in gymnasiums and schoolyards trying to perfect the rudiments of a game that remains simple to this day. The game was invented as a diversion, but for many youths it is a way of life.

Stories abound of superstars who spent their childhoods perfecting their game in total disregard of the elements. Walt Frazier learned to dribble on a rocky schoolyard in Atlanta, Jerry West swished jump shots in the darkness of rural West Virginia, and Connie Hawkins (who once said, "Basketball was my first love") created his moves against the tough competition in the playgrounds of a Brooklyn ghetto.

All professional basketball players put in long, hard hours of practice, but for them, as it is with budding 12-year-old superstars, the fun and challenge of basketball remains the game itself. It is the platform where players' abilities and egos clash. The long hours of toil and repetition end when the game begins.

LET'S KEEP SCORE

The object of basketball, of course, is to win. That's why the score is kept. Everything is directed to that end—the strategy, the workouts, the training, and, particularly on the collegiate and professional levels, the publicity buildup that brings the fan into the arena. It is the basic tenet of the game, as it is with most games, and it is foremost at every level, from junior YMCA leagues to the big leagues.

If winning didn't matter, basketball never would have attained its present level of acceptance, not only in this country but abroad as well. Not long ago, someone suggested basketball be played as an art form—like a ballet—and that no score and no statistics be kept. This revolutionary idea would eliminate many of the physical and mental pressures a player must endure, but it would also strip the game of its attraction and resources. The fundamental individual challenge, one-on-one basketball, breeds the competition that fascinates the public. Without it, basketball would not be a sport and it would draw about as much attention as a hand of solitaire.

But just as fundamental is the fact that you won't win all the time. Even Kareem Abdul-Jabbar, a player of extraordinary ability, knows what it is like to lose.

During the middle of the 1974-75 season, a very bad one for the

(Facing page.) Kareem Abdul-Jabbar shoots his skyhook. He is so accurate with this shot that he is practically impossible to stop. Notice he has great fingertip control as he releases the ball.

Los Angeles Lakers, I encountered my great college coach John Wooden at a drugstore in Westwood, the site of UCLA. After exchanging pleasantries, I complained about how poorly our team was doing. He listened intently, as usual. Soon his paternal smile appeared. "Just be thankful you haven't had to go through it more often," he told me. "There are some who have had to go through it many more times than you."

Losing plays a big part in basketball and players must adapt to it. I believe that to truly enjoy victory you must have had to endure defeat. A player must know the sensation of walking off the court a loser, knowing he was beaten because the other guy was better that night, as well as the sensation of walking off the floor a winner. As a player, you should accept the challenge of a loss. Try to understand why you lost and what went wrong, so you can make corrections and improve your game for the future. Once you have done that, you are further along to being a successful basketball player.

Whereas winning lies at the heart of the game, it is not the only criterion for success. There is the individual aspect to be considered. A player is successful when he fulfills his potential and uses his ability to further the team effort on the playing floor. Coach Wooden, who won 10 national championships at UCLA, always told his players that if they played as hard and as well as they possibly could, the end result would take care of itself.

Not everyone can play on a winning team, so you must be able to take satisfaction in your own performance. This doesn't mean you rush over to the scorer's table at the end of the game to see how many points you've scored. Scoring is important, but so are rebounding, passing, and defense. As an individual, you must mold your talents with the others so that the team is solid and working with precision. If you have done your part, and done it well, then you can be proud, regardless of the outcome.

Basketball is a game of habits and instincts. Once the game begins, the players attempt to accomplish what was prepared for in practice and to react to what is happening on the floor. It is like driving a car or riding a bike. You simply know how to play. Your instincts take over and you become capable of making instantaneous decisions without ever mulling over the advantages and disadvantages. Of course, there will be times when you wish you had a second or two to decide, particularly after an overhead pass, which should have slipped through the defense, is picked off by a defender. But if you have sound habits and instincts, the decision you make usually will be the right one.

A player should be emotionally and physically ready for every game, since theoretically each is as important as the next. In high school or college that goal might be realistic, since schedules rarely consist of more than 30 games, but in the NBA, where there is a minimum of 82, players sometimes have a tendency to overlook a game that they feel is unimportant. Sometimes it depends on the opponent and where your team is ranked in the standings. It's only natural to be more emotionally charged for a big game before a packed house in Madison Square Garden than for a meaningless affair before a couple of thousand people in Hofheinz Pavilion in Houston. That's no excuse, however. Regardless of the rigorous schedule, players always should be prepared. But players can be unpredictable. I have gone into games feeling great and had terrible nights, while on the other hand I have had great games on nights when I felt lethargic. But the player has an obligation to play as well as he can. He owes that not only to himself, but also to his team and to the fans.

In a way, professional basketball has caught up with the colleges in that there now is more stress placed on team play. When the league first started, it promoted individuals, the superstars like Bob Cousy, George Mikan, Bill Russell, Wilt Chamberlain, Elgin Baylor, Oscar Robertson, and Jerry West. The superstars were a vehicle for the league to survive, but now that professional basketball has achieved a level of success, fans come out to see the great teams as well as the great individuals.

It is understood, as Golden State proved in winning the NBA championship, that a team has a better chance of winning if all players are involved in the game. The individual must be subordinate to the team. Rarely will one player, even if he is a superstar, win consistently. He may make a major contribution, possibly greater than the sum of the others, but it must be within the framework of the team. As a player, you should realize your abilities and those of your

The two greatest guards ever to play the game are Jerry West (with the ball) and Oscar Robertson (guarding him). Jerry shows great body balance as he stops and prepares to go up for the jump shot. His right foot is firmly planted, his knees are bent, his head is up, and the ball is protected.

teammates and understand the roles each has been designated to play.

All players are aware of their own talents despite the team. Everyone wants to play. If you play and play well, the chances of furthering your career are greater. In the pros, there are greater personal rewards. So the team concept is somewhat undermined because the individual has his own ambitions to satisfy. However, if the team wins and everyone plays to their ability, everyone receives a share of the exposure, the fame, and the satisfaction.

GAME DAY

Everyone has his own methods of preparing for a game. Some will follow a strict regimen while others will act as though it's just another day. No one knows what is best, although coaches and trainers will have their own preferences. You should do whatever suits you, but keep in mind that it is important to be well rested. I would discourage doing anything fatiguing the day of a game.

If you are in school, your day already will be structured. You have to be at school at a certain time and you have classes to attend. In the pros, it is different. Unless we are traveling, we have the entire day to prepare.

Playing for the Los Angeles Lakers under Bill Sharman, we have what he calls the "shoot-around" the day of a game. There are no exceptions unless we are traveling or, I suppose, there is a natural disaster. But the latter never has been tested.

The shoot-around consists of loosening-up exercises, jump shots, layins, and three-man fast-break drills. It usually begins at 11 A.M. and lasts for 30 minutes or more, depending upon the availability of scouting films, in which case they are watched after the shoot-around.

Sharman initiated the shoot-around and, much to the chagrin of many players throughout the league, it has become very popular. He does it for two reasons.

First, he wants his players to have a feel for the ball and a feel for the court that particular day. Unfortunately, he sometimes is thwarted because on game mornings he can't schedule the arena we're going to play in that night. In that case, he will find another gym. He doesn't want us running hard, he just wants basketball running through our systems.

Second, he wants us out of bed at a decent hour and into a routine. He figures the players will be sluggish for the game if they sleep all day, which some players would do. He would rather have us active than spending the day hanging around our hotel rooms.

At UCLA, Wooden never had a shoot-around. He feared that his players might leave their games in the gym in the morning.

I don't run hard at a shoot-around. I just concentrate on shooting for 20 or 30 minutes and that's it. I don't particularly like the shoot-around, but overall I think it has helped. I know it hasn't hurt my game. During the last few years I have shot as well as, or better than, I have in any other period in my career.

Afterwards we might watch the scouting film or spend a few minutes walking through the plays of our opponent—which will make us aware of the team we are to play that night. This session actually provides us ample time to think about our opponent. I try not to concentrate on the game until later. You can't dwell on the game all day because it will drive you batty.

When Sharman finally lets us go, I'll have lunch. Usually it will be just a snack, especially if I had breakfast before the shoot-around. Then I'll relax during the afternoon. I'll run a few errands and take care of some business, but nothing too serious. Or, if I'm on the road, I may go to a movie. Basically, I try to stay loose and keep my head clear.

My pregame meal, which I'll have about three and a half hours before the game, is unorthodox. The traditional view is to eat plenty of protein, particularly beef, but I eat carbohydrates—foods like pancakes, waffles, and spaghetti. Carbohydrates give you energy, which burns up quickly once the game starts. If you are active, as all basketball players are, carbohydrates won't lie in your stomach. Protein is good too, but the energy it provides won't benefit you until the next day or the day after.

Many players are not overly concerned with the pregame meal; in fact, some have sent a ball boy out for hot dogs right before the game. Again, everyone has his own methods of preparing for a game. Being a small man in a big man's game, however, I'm always seeking an edge, and I believe a proper diet is important. If you feel that eating carbohydrates for your pregame meal is too unusual, I suggest you discuss the matter with several qualified nutritionists and devise a diet of your own.

When I played for John Wooden at UCLA, he always insisted that we go to our rooms and nap before leaving as a team for the game. He wanted us rested. This is a practice I've continued ever since. After my pregame meal, I religiously take my nap. If I can't sleep, then I'll just rest in bed. I don't know if this helps my play, but I have found that I feel better if I do.

For an 8 o'clock game, I get up around 5:30, take my time dressing, and leave for the game at 6. Then I start thinking about the game and the players I will face.

Having been in the NBA for 11 years, I know the other players. I know their styles and habits and I adapt my game accordingly. This knowledge is gained through experience and scouting reports. At the high school and college levels, you may have an idea of what the opposition likes to do, but the information usually isn't as detailed. If you do have the information, though, take advantage of it.

I have learned that players usually will do what they do best. This doesn't mean they won't surprise you. A good player will be versatile, so you must guard against all possibilities. Still, you will be more conscious of his strengths.

I think about a player's moves, what he likes to do on offense, and how I might expect him to play me. Nate Archibald is known and respected for his ability to penetrate, but he is a good outside shooter and an excellent passer. Walt Frazier is a strong defensive player who can also shoot, pass, and run. You can go down the list of all the players in the NBA and grade what they do best and you will have the information that most of the players in the league already have.

If you rate me as a ball player, the first thing that comes to mind is that I can score. I think I shoot the ball better than I pass, but I pass well, too. I have been criticized for my defense, which I believe is unjustified, for I play better defense than most experts give me credit for. My size may be an obstacle, but you don't see too many players scoring 30 points off me. On the drive, I'm more effective going to my left, but I also move well to the right and can pull up at any time for the jump shot.

If we're to play Kansas City, I will prepare myself to play Archibald. Here are some of the things that will run through my mind.

Nate is a very explosive player, particularly if the game breaks wide open. Once he starts fast-breaking there isn't much you can do because he'll charge down court in the center of the break and pass the ball all over the floor. You must try to slow him down and keep him from controlling the tempo.

I try to shade him to his right on defense. I also want help from my teammates. The only way you can afford to play him straight up is if you are as quick as he, and few in the league are. If you allow him to go both ways, you will be in for a long, hectic evening because he can go to his left and his right equally well. Although he has improved his outside shooting considerably in recent years, you would rather have him firing away from there than penetrating and feeding off. He will still get his points, which can't be prevented unless he is unusually cold, but it will be more difficult for him to have the real big night, the 30- or 40-pointer. Also, you make a mental note to keep him off the foul line. Because he drives so frequently, he shoots a lot of free throws and he can kill you from there.

From an offensive point of view, I'm aware that some defenders guard the jump shooter better and others the driver. Archibald belongs in the latter category. He is one of the few players in the league I'm taller than, so when I play against him I will try to get in a position where I can just shoot the ball. I don't worry about him blocking my shot. If I can get the ball within my range, I'll just turn and shoot over him.

I won't force the drive for two reasons. First, if I have a 15-, 18-, or 20-foot jump shot, I'll take it. I feel I can hit the longer ones as well. Second, I must be wary of Nate taking the charge. He is so quick and clever that he's able to get set and take away my lane. The drive would only put me into foul trouble—which I always try to avoid.

Like Nate, Jerry Sloan of Chicago also looks for the charge. Even though he is 6-foot-5, I'll be working for the jump shot when I play him. He goes for the charge every time. You don't even have to touch him and he'll fall down. I can't play both men the same way.

Nate Archibald drives past two of my former teammates, Keith Erickson (right) and Mel Counts, on his way to the basket. He is the best penetrating guard playing the game today.

Jerry West (left) and Jerry Sloan battle for a rebound under the basket. Sloan, a rugged and great defensive player, plays with a great deal of intensity and has gotten the maximum out of his ability. He comes to play every night.

Against Archibald, I sometimes am able to post him, back him in a bit, and turn and shoot over him. I can't do that against Sloan. Not only is he stronger and taller, but putting the ball on the floor would be playing into his strength, which is unwise. Since I'm quicker, I will work harder without the ball trying to get the open jump shot.

Walt Frazier of New York and Phil Chenier of Washington, who are similar defensively, present different problems. Unlike Archibald and Sloan, these two look for the steal rather than the charge. They are gamblers. I have learned it's foolish to try to beat either on the dribble, for that is playing into their strength. Instead, the key is to move without the ball and, when I receive it, make my move quickly. Both are smart ball players and play excellent position, but the fact that they usually look for the steal or to help out their teammates enables me to sometimes capitalize on their gambles.

Besides the actual experience of playing against a man, another good way to study an opponent is through the use of film. I spent a lot of time last summer researching the previous season's game films. It is tedious but invaluable work. You not only can analyze others' play, but you can study your own. You can spot mistakes you weren't aware you were making during the game.

I was first exposed to films when I was in high school. My coach had a few of our games filmed, but I was so intrigued with seeing myself on the silver screen that I only noticed what I was doing right and not what I was doing wrong. Now, however, I am much more critical, as I am looking for mistakes. I will be watching the film and all of a sudden I will say to myself, "Hey, what am I doing standing there? I should be moving." You just don't realize you are standing at the time.

At the college and high school levels, films sometimes are not available, but if they are, you should take advantage of them.

Whomever I play, whether it is a veteran like Sloan or a young rookie, I get mentally ready for a game. I have learned to respect all players. After all, all those playing on the same court have attained the same level of achievement. Some are better than others, but all are capable of beating you on any night. Overconfidence has led to many upsets. I think the Washington Bullets can attest to that. They were heavy favorites to beat Golden State for the NBA championship in the 1974-75 season and undoubtedly they believed they would win with little difficulty. But the Warriors played well and their confidence mounted as the series moved along. Washington never did break out of its sluggishness.

The Lakers' championship team of 1972 was a very confident basketball team, but it respected the opposition. We happened to be so strong, and we had so much talent, that we believed we could turn it on at will, which we did frequently. Our confidence reached incredible heights, particularly during our 33-game winning streak. Rarely, however, will a team, on any level, be that imposing.

Confidence is a strong force in basketball as it is in other facets of life. Without it, you can't expect to win. Many players have possessed more ability than I, but I believe the success I have had can be attributed to determination and the desire to win. It is a confidence that borders on cockiness. I try not to be cocky, but when you are super-confident it sometimes appears that way.

During my career, I have tried to borrow much of coach John Wooden's philosophy. "Be confident, but never cocky," he would always say. So I try to play with confidence and I think it has made me a little better than some of the other players. When I go out on the floor, I just don't figure on losing. Of course, I realize I will at times but I won't submit easily.

In the locker room before the game we will begin to discuss the game as a team. We will discuss the players expected to start for the opposition and rehash their favorite moves and what the team will set up for them. You can expect every team to gear its plays and style to what its players do best. We try to break up those plans and we discuss ways of doing so during our pregame meeting.

Chicago, for example, would always try to get the ball to its shooters, Chet Walker and Bob Love. Our forwards would then be told that Chet liked to put the ball on the floor once or twice, pull up, give you the head-and-shoulder fake, and shoot. The Bulls always ran a few plays for Walker. One would result in his receiving the ball at a particular spot on the left side of the basket, so coach Sharman would tell our forwards to try to prevent him from receiving the ball where he wanted to. If we were successful at that, we took a part of Chicago's offense away, which gave us a big edge.

You should remember that most players like certain spots on the floor from which to shoot. They also favor certain patterns because of the timing and execution. If your coach points this information out to you, be aware of it during the game. Nothing is more frustrating than a defender who prevents you from roaming where you wish on the floor.

After discussing each player, we will move into the team aspect. Against the Bulls, you have to run. You must take them out of their movement, because they run their patterns well and with great patience. Since they like to initiate their plays with a pass to the forward, we'll try to take that away and force the initial pass into the center. Boston, on the other hand, is a running team, so coach Sharman will stress slowing the cutters. What he means is that we should have a hand, a feel, or a touch on them at all times. This tactic may be illegal in high school and college, but it is allowed in the pros. He doesn't want us to stray too far away from our men. Against some teams we'll concede the outside shot while against others we'll attempt to force the drive. When the New York Knicks had great outside shooters during the early 1970s, we tried to guard them closely. We wanted them to take the ball to the hoop where we had Wilt Chamberlain plugging up the defense. Sharman always reminds us of the characteristics of the team we are up against that night and then sums up the meeting with a few generalities like "We have to fast-break them . . . we have to beat them on the boards. . . ."

If you get ready for every game the way in theory it should be done, all games become equally important. When the big one rolls around it will be like any other because you already have been disciplined and prepared. The pressure shouldn't affect you.

I have found pressure is constructed by the media and spectators. Don't compound it by putting more pressure on yourself. Take an NBA championship series game. The players will continue to do the same things they have done all season. The same habits will be present, the teams will have played almost 100 games each, and they will have met one another maybe six times. By then, the players will know their opponents almost as well as they know their teammates. Under those conditions there can't be many surprises. Coaches are reluctant to change a team's style of play that late in the season, so everyone knows what to expect.

You must block out the press and the pressure it builds. If you are in high school or college, you must block out the influence of friends and family. That is why I say you can't think about the game all the time. To sit in your room and dwell upon it will make you tight and tense when the game finally begins. There is only so much you can think about anyway. You must be physically and mentally sharp for a game. One of the most significant lessons a person can learn from athletics is to make decisions firmly and quickly under emotional strain.

THE TEAM

At all positions on the basketball court, your team should have players who can score, rebound, run, handle the ball, and play defense. In the vernacular of sports, you want players who "can do it all." But Rick Barrys and Kareem Abdul-Jabbars are rare. Consequently, basketball has become specialized in recent years and the ingredients necessary to win have come into focus.

The essential, but minimum, requirements are two men to rebound, three to score—and a guard who can quarterback. Here's how it breaks down by position.

In the backcourt one of the guards must be the playmaker. It is his responsibility to work the ball to the scorers, set up plays, and control the tempo of the game. He is the quarterback. He should have sound basketball sense. He should recognize the player with the hot hand and make sure he gets the ball. But he also should be aware of the others. Everyone wants to be involved in the offense, so it is the playmaker's responsibility that all get the opportunity to score.

Some of the better playmakers in the NBA today are Kevin Porter of Detroit, who led the league in assists in 1974-75 when with Washington, Ernie DiGregorio of Buffalo, Norm Van Lier of Chicago, and Walt Frazier of the Knicks.

The other guard should be primarily a scorer, although he must be able to handle the ball and initiate plays when called upon. As a scorer, he should be expert in the art of shooting. The team relies on him to put points on the board, so he must be consistent and deadly.

Detroit's playmaking guard Kevin Porter is always on the move, and sets the tempo for his team.

Here's West the passer and Goodrich the shooter. Laker coach Bill Sharman paid us a great compliment by saying we comprised the best back-court combination he had ever seen.

Everyone will have cold nights occasionally, but the shooter can't afford them too often.

Chenier of the Bullets, Geoff Petrie of Portland, and Fred Brown of Seattle are among the top shooting guards in the league. All are pure shooters with long range.

Jerry West and I, I believe, were examples of a strong backcourt when we played together for the Lakers in the early 70s. West was the playmaker and I was the scorer. (West was also a great shooter.) Frazier and Earl Monroe make up a strong backcourt for the Knicks, as do Chenier and Dave Bing for the Bullets and Jo Jo White and Charlie Scott for Boston.

The third guard must be a jack of all trades. He should be able to score, set up plays, and play defense. At one time or another, he will replace both guards, so an all-around talent is required. All guards should be adequate defensively, at the minimum, but if one of the starters is weak, the other had better be strong.

John Havlicek was the third guard for the Celtics for years and did an excellent job in sparking the team whenever he entered the game. He was a good example of a third guard who could play all facets of the position well. Jimmy Jones of Washington, a top guard in the ABA before he joined the Bullets, is one of the better third guards in the NBA today, as is Gus Williams of the Golden State Warriors.

Up front, one of the forwards should be a scorer and the other a rebounder. You can't win consistently with all the scoring coming from the outside. The forwards are close to the basket, so it is mandatory that the team get points from there. A balanced scoring attack is preferred, but in lieu of that, there must be an offensive threat from the corner. Essentially, he is the balance to the scoring guard. The strong-side forward must rebound with the center, as the latter needs help on the boards if the team is to get its share of rebounds.

Among the better scoring forwards are Rick Barry, John Havlicek, Sidney Wicks, and George McGinnis. Dave DeBusschere, one of the best rebounding forwards in the game before his retirement, teamed with Bill Bradley to give the Knicks a well-balanced front line when they were champions and contenders through the early 1970s. Now, some of the better strong rebounding forwards are Elvin Hayes of Washington, Paul Silas of Boston, and Jim Brewer of Cleveland.

Connie Hawkins once was asked about the importance of the center. "Why do you think they call him the center?" he asked before answering the question. "Because he's the center of attraction out

Golden State's Rick Barry is the league's premier forward. As they say, he can do it all. Here he uses the old-fashioned underhand method, which has made him the best free-throw shooter.

there." The center is the hub of the wheel on both offense and defense.

He must be a rebounder. He plays around the basket, so it is important that he keep the ball alive. He isn't required to score much if both forwards are involved in the offense, which Bill Russell proved, but it is desirable that he be capable of scoring because of his proximity to the hoop. A clever center will get numerous high-percentage shots, forcing the defense to collapse in the middle, thus opening up the offense outside.

The center doesn't necessarily have to be a shot blocker, but he should be a good defender. Being in the middle, he is responsible for helping teammates who get beat. He must prevent the opposition from scoring many points close to the basket.

A passing center is a considerable asset; he gives a team flexibility and enhances the offense. He can come out high, he can play low, he can swing from one side to the other, and he can be particularly effective in hitting the cutters. To fast-break, the center must be adept at picking the ball off the defensive board and whipping it down court quickly and accurately. If the center can only shoot, eventually the defense will collapse on him, forcing the bad shot or forcing him to kick the ball backcourt, thus delaying the offense.

The great centers over the years have been excellent passers. Kareem Abdul-Jabbar, Dave Cowens, and Bill Walton are the best passing centers in the game today besides being tremendous scorers, defenders, and rebounders. Other top centers are Bob McAdoo of Buffalo and Bob Lanier of Detroit, both great scorers.

Many big men come into professional basketball today unable to handle the ball properly because coaches on the high school and college levels don't teach them. They want points out of the big center, which is fine. They fail to realize, however, the value of the center's ability to pass the ball. Not only will he help the team, but he will grow more as a basketball player.

Since there is an abundance of talent in the game today, rarely will one man dominate. Even a superstar like Abdul-Jabbar needs help from four teammates who are well versed in the fundamentals. The ideal setting requires that all players share in the scoring, rebounding, and passing. An opponent will find such a team difficult to

Boston's center, Dave Cowens, plays what I call "the entire game."
He scores, he rebounds, he runs, he plays the "D," and, above all,
he hustles all the time. Here he tips one in against Kareem Abdul-
Jabbar.

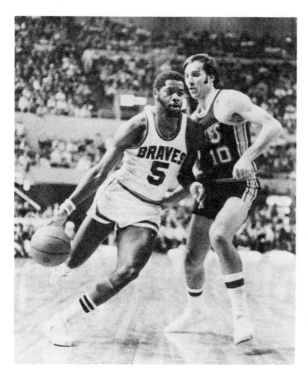

Buffalo's Jim Mc-Millian, who played on the Lakers' 1971-72 championship team, plays with what coaches term intelligence. He has excellent court instincts and anticipation.

defend. A player's talents won't be distributed evenly among the various areas of the game, but he is expected to contribute in all facets. A great shooter must play some defense; a great rebounder must handle the ball at times; a great defender must rebound; and a great rebounder must know how to handle the ball.

PLAY WITH INTELLIGENCE

Despite its being an overworked term, "playing with intelligence" exists and is inherent in winners. It is the ability to assess a situation and react accordingly. Since basketball is such a fast-paced game, a player must adjust constantly on the floor. Once the game begins, he doesn't have time to stop and evaluate what is happening.

Taking a positive attitude will help. If you believe you can do something better the next time you try it, you will become smarter and acquire a better feel for the game. If you are a good shooter and you only get five shots a game, there is a reason for it. The defense may be tough, but perhaps you weren't working hard enough without the ball and didn't create opportunities for yourself. You must assume part of the blame and be more aggressive in the future. If your man scores 30 points, there is a reason for that, too. It takes a positive attitude to analyze a negative situation and overcome the adversity. Since it is a team game, there will be several reasons, but you, as an individual, must assume your share of the blame and subsequently rectify it.

Knowledge is not easily acquired, but you can increase your awareness by knowing the rules of the game, being imaginative in your tactics, and gaining a psychological and physical edge through intimidation of your opponent.

The least a basketball player should know is the rules of the game. Yet games have been lost because one player carelessly called for time after all timeouts were used, held the ball for longer than five seconds while attempting to put the ball in bounds, failed to notify the scorekeeper before entering the game as a substitute, took longer than ten seconds to shoot a free throw, or entered the lane before the ball left the hands of the free-throw shooter.

All the above are careless mistakes and can be avoided by a thorough knowledge and awareness of the rules. Read a rulebook carefully and be cognizant of any changes that may affect the league in which you play. Consult a coach if you have any questions.

The variables in basketball are infinite and if you are to succeed you must be on top of them all, or at least most of them. You must know instinctively what to do at the right time. Much of your tactical knowledge will come through experience, but good coaching, particularly in high school and college, is invaluable. The coach can point out tactical nuances that ordinarily might be overlooked.

Here are some examples of tactical situations to look for:

—If a teammate has a hot hand, go to him. The object is to score points, so the ball must get to the man who can put the ball in the basket.

—If there's a defensive weakness, take advantage of it. There is no room in basketball for charity. If an opponent can't do the job, recognize it quickly and concentrate your attack in his area.

—If a teammate is getting beat defensively, be ready to help out. Keep an eye on your man, though, because he can take advantage of your helping out.

—If you are coming down the center on a three-on-two break, assess the defensive setup quickly and carefully before making the play. If you wait too long, you may lose the advantage; if you make the wrong decision you may end up with a poor-percentage shot or no shot at all.

—If a teammate's offensive strength is the jump shot, make yourself available for screens. The screen, when executed properly, is a potent weapon. Not only will it free a man for the jump shot, it will create the pick and roll, a basic and effective two-on-two situation.

—If you were open for a shot and didn't get the pass, don't pout. Everyone is missed at times and you must accept it. Your teammate won't pass you up on purpose. If he does, then your team has problems that extend beyond the playing floor. Probably he just didn't see you or couldn't make the pass. Sometimes the passing angle is deceptive, depending upon where you are on the floor. But keep moving, because even though you were missed that time, you may be open a second or two later.

—If your opponent has position on the boards, try to out-maneuver him. Often the rebound will go to the aggressive rebounder. Paul Silas, one of the best rebounding forwards in the NBA, isn't a big jumper. He attributes his success to shrewdness. Being so quick, he often manages to slip into position while the defender is following the flight of the ball.

—If your man is having a big night, make adjustments in your defense. If he has made two or three straight 15-footers, take that shot away. Apply more pressure and force him out farther.

—If your shot is off, make adjustments. Your errant shooting can be disastrous to the team, so you may have to drive in order to get to the free-throw line. Sometimes it will take a few free throws or a few easy baskets for you to regain your rhythm and confidence.

A player is responsible for his own play. He can influence the movement of the other nine men on the floor, and in doing so he constantly must adjust his tactical approach to the flow of the game.

A psychological edge can be gained by accomplished ball stealers like Slick Watts and Rick Barry, strong physical rebounders like Paul Silas, and shot-blocking centers like Kareem Abdul-Jabbar.

Usually intimidation is associated with the bigger and stronger players, but guards can be intimidating also. Jerry West, who was 6-foot-4 and weighed 190 pounds when he played, intimidated opponents through sheer quickness and intelligence. A jump shot was a precarious adventure when he was on the court. He perfected the ploy of slipping behind a shooter and deflecting the ball from the rear. Consequently, shooters would go up for a shot with one eye on the basket and the other looking for West.

He also made opponents shudder when he had control of the ball near the end of a tight game. His last-second heroics are legendary. He was capable of unnerving opponents just by his presence in crucial situations.

Not everyone can be a Jerry West, of course, but you can be an intimidating force if you perform coolly and intelligently at critical junctures of the game. One who consistently makes the "big play" is a great player.

There is nothing more discouraging than having a smoothly executed drive wind up with the ball spiked into the first row or into the hands of an opponent. It tends to induce neurosis. If you have the ability to block shots, use it, but don't sacrifice other parts of your game for the glory of the block.

Regarding the dangers inherent in being intimidated, there is just one rule: Don't be. You lose your effectiveness as a basketball player if you do. We know that basketball is a noncontact sport, but we also know that that is a fallacy, an anachronism from gentler times. There is a great deal of contact in basketball at all levels and there is no indication that it will diminish. You might ask yourself how badly you want to play the game. To succeed in basketball you must play at

100 percent, and fear takes a healthy cut from that number.

Having a shot blocked can be embarrassing, but don't allow it to be intimidating. Maybe the other fellow made a sensational play, or perhaps it was merely a bad shot. In either case, don't be afraid to make the play again. Only next time, put more arch on the shot or make a quicker move to the basket.

The drive should be a significant part of your game, since all of your offense can't come from the outside. A one-dimensional offensive threat is no threat at all. Besides, penetration not only adds variety to your game, it creates opportunities for your team and probably will give you more opportunities to go to the free-throw line. If you are even slightly intimidated, to the degree that you won't drive against certain players, your play suffers.

A blocked shot is a blocked shot and that is all. Again, a positive outlook is required. I prefer the word "respect" over the word "intimidation," actually. I respect a player who blocks shots, but I'm not intimidated. Bill Russell, one of the most respected and feared players in the history of the game, did not frighten me. He blocked some of my shots (and I'm still looking for some of them) but I never stopped driving on him. After you have had the shot blocked, the test is to drive on the man, create the play again and put the ball through the hoop.

Playing basketball with intelligence is a composite of common sense, flexibility, adaptability, intuition, and grit. It is difficult to teach, but easy to recognize. You can see it in all great players on winning teams.

TEMPO

There are two basic offensive theories in basketball, both of which affect the tempo of the game. The first is a patterned or slow-down offense and the second is fast-break. Having played for John Wooden at UCLA and for Bill Sharman with the Lakers, I am a fervent proponent of the latter. Although teams on many levels of the game play the fast break, it particularly is embodied in professional basketball.

When the NBA introduced the 24-second clock in 1954, it permanently altered the makeup of basketball. The beat of the game, once patient and relaxed, became more lively. It gave the sport a shot in the arm. Patience still is a virtue, but no longer is it the only one. With a time limit of 24 seconds to shoot the ball imposed on the offense, a team cannot afford to relax. A 10- or 12-point lead can vanish in a minute.

The principal casualty of the 24-second rule was the stall or delayed game, a strategy that remains effective on all levels of basketball other than the professional. Basically, it is used to waste time and protect leads, which is the very reason the pros discarded it. But Pete Newell, now general manager of the Lakers, once had one of his players hold the ball for 12 full minutes. He was coach of the University of California, Berkeley, then and he was playing Bill Russell and the University of San Francisco, a team that won two National Collegiate Athletic Association titles and 60 straight games. Newell's team was behind by just a few points to the superior USF team when he employed the stall. He figured his team would have a better chance of winning if they played fewer minutes. They played fewer minutes and Newell's team still lost, but he defends his decision to this day.

Many college coaches would prefer a 30-second rule, which also would effectively eliminate the stall—but all have a stall in their offensive repertoire, anyway. It may be unexciting and it may slow the tempo, but the stall has won many games and should be used at the right time if allowed.

To control the tempo, you must know when to run and when to slow down; when to press and when to call it off; when to call time out and when to wait. These decisions must be made correctly if your team is to seize the momentum of the game.

If your opponent is playing well, call time out. Slow play down and set up your offense. Tighten your defense and be more aggressive. Whatever you do, don't panic. Just put the game in its proper perspective and take control of your play. The better you control the tempo, the better your chances of winning the game. During time-outs, discuss what must be done—rebound, get the ball off the boards and down court, defense, and call a play to get a quick basket. To change the tempo in your favor, adjustments must be made immediately. Otherwise the game may get out of hand.

Once adjustments are made, you may get back into the game. Instead of being down by eight points, you may be down by two and at that juncture it becomes a new game. Get your offense flowing properly—movement, passing, and hitting the open man—and begin taking the four-on-threes and the five-on-fours. Take good high-percentage shots. On the break, pass up the 20-footer for the 15-footer or the drive.

Of course, much will depend on your team's style of play. The Chicago Bulls, for example, set up exceptionally well with a patterned offense. They don't want the game to get scattered and will try to lull you to sleep. It is difficult for a basketball team to turn the momentum off and on at will, but if it can it will be a good one.

Oftentimes, a team will control the tempo through the first half and hold a large lead at halftime, only to blow all or most of it during the first few minutes of the second. Complacency and a loss of mental toughness are the causes. Over a long season, it is sometimes easy for a player or team to take one game for granted—especially after taking a commanding and easy lead. The losing team, meanwhile, may start the second half tough and aggressive after being humiliated in the first half. And once they get off to a good start, the momentum, which has swung their way, will be difficult to recover.

Half time is a respite, but it is also a period for reflection and mental preparation. No matter what the score, you must stay in the game. There are reasons for a team's playing well, so during the halftime intermission, rehash what you did so it can continue in the second half. Guard against relaxing.

Conversely, it becomes tempting for a player or team to submit after falling behind by 20 points. But that is precisely when you should accept the challenge. You can't do anything about the past, but you can improve the future. Basically you are accepting the same challenge throughout the game. What are six or eight points? Three field goals and a couple of free throws. A team can make up that margin quickly. A three-point play, a steal and a basket, a defensive rebound, and a fast break layin—and you're down by one. It is easily erased. Twenty points is harder, naturally, but you can come back from that, too, if you prepare yourself properly and make your move slowly but steadily. You can't expect to overcome a 20-point deficit all at once.

Detractors of professional basketball usually will say that games are always decided during the last two minutes. That often is true, but I have found that the tempo continually is a major part of the game. You will find out the final score if you arrive for the last two minutes, but you will miss the previous 46 minutes in which the game builds momentum to reach that point.

There are three critical stages in a game: the first six minutes, the first few minutes of the third quarter, and the last few minutes—if the game is still in doubt.

The initial tempo is set soon after the game begins. If you start out flat, chances are you will be playing catch-up ball all game. Under those circumstances, it is difficult to win. The same is true after half time. If you can score two or three quick baskets, either you are back in a game you were out of, or you can pull ahead from a tight one. The last two or three minutes decide a game when the score is close. The defense gets tougher and the players tired. Still, the team that wins will be the one that makes the important baskets and comes up with the big plays during this period.

No one was better in the last two minutes than Jerry West. He accepted the challenge and enjoyed being in the position of winning or losing for his team. He always said he wanted the ball in critical situations. It was part of his make-up as a player. He wanted to take the last shot or go to the free-throw line. I like to think I have that quality, too. It takes tremendous self-confidence, as you must believe you can put the ball in the basket when victory or defeat is on the line. You can't make the shot all the time, but you should be able to make it more often than not. It isn't always the shot that is critical, however. Sometimes it is a rebound, a pass, or a key defensive play. Try to be the player who can make the big play. It's a quality all great players possess.

To control the tempo, a team must have movement—which is as essential to the game as the ball itself. The player who stands still is easy to guard, while the one who moves is difficult.

It is very logical. Standing in one place not only clogs up your offense, it allows the defender to help his teammates. The defender knows you must have the ball in the area in which you are standing. But if you're moving, he must move. Proper movement is not simply moving, either. You must move with a purpose, within the framework of your team's offense. Plays are designed so that your movement—a screen, a pass, a dribble—will free a teammate for a high-percentage shot.

The more movement a team has, the easier it becomes to free a man for a shot. If I'm one-on-one with my defender, I can either shoot from where I am or drive. But if there is a screen, another option opens up. It gives the defense something else to worry about. The defender either must go over it, go around it, or switch. Whatever he decides to do, he will lose a half-step—if it is executed properly.

The tempo, the essential beat of the game, ultimately will be controlled by one team—the winning one. You try to intimidate your opponent and seize the tempo with fluid movement at the beginning, then make adjustments during half time and implement them early in the second half, and, finally, you reach back for that extra effort, for the big play, if necessary, at the end.

PLAY WITH POISE

How good it feels to occasionally blow your stack, call an official a blankety-blank, and gesture wildly to the fans. But what does it get you? A technical foul, maybe two, and ejection from the game. The official doesn't lose, neither does the fan. Only you . . . and your team.

Maintaining control of your emotions is important for two principal reasons. First, you must think clearly to make the right decisions on the basketball floor; and second, technical fouls will cost the team points plus your services—which are valuable.

It is difficult for a player to realize that he will never change an official's call. I know, it took me years. I used to figure complaining would help me on the next call, but it doesn't. I sincerely believe the referees will call a game honestly, but they will miss calls because the game is so fast and the players so big that it is practically impossible for them to make all the correct calls. Arguing won't help matters. If

Walt Frazier, sometimes referred to as "Mr. Cool," slips through the Laker defense for an easy jump shot. He plays with a great deal of poise and is there to make the big play in the final two minutes.

anything, it will alienate you from the officials. Even if you are right, it won't help, so accept the calls stoically.

Regarding the fans: the fact that they pay to see the game allows them some freedom of expression, barring physical attacks upon the participants. For the most part, they attend games to root for the home team and malign the opponent. As a visitor, then, you must learn to maintain your level of ability despite the taunts from the crowd. You are subject to the whims of the fans and they will ride you, particularly if you are a quality or controversial player. They will try to upset you, and the best way to quiet them is to play good basketball.

Anything that disturbs your concentration will disrupt your effectiveness as a player. You will make errors you normally would not make if you allow your composure to crumble because of an official's call or the heckling of a crowd. Take it in stride and remain cool inside.

COMING OFF THE BENCH

On every team, unfortunately, some players will spend much of the time on the bench. From my point of view, it is the most bewildering role in the game. I have never adapted well to it and I have found this to be true with others. Somehow, you must keep happy, in shape, and in tune with your teammates. Everyone wants to play, but not everyone can. That's just a fact of life when you have 10, 11, or 12 men on a team.

For the welfare of the team, the first rule is not to sulk. The second is to stay alert and keep your mind on the game so that when you are called upon to play, you can contribute immediately. A substitute can't relax and enjoy the game as a spectator would. Early in his career, John Havlicek was the archetypal sixth man. As soon as he entered the game, he would contribute. He would score, make a steal, make a key pass, or grab a rebound. He joined the flow of the game immediately, as he was keenly aware that a key reserve didn't have the luxury of four or five minutes of warm-ups.

Since starters usually don't play the entire game, the third guard, third forward, and backup center are prominent positions. Their

John Havlicek, the highest-scoring active player, hits another two against the Lakers. John's an example of a player who always is ready to play. Early in his career he was Boston's valuable sixth man who sparked the team coming off the bench.

task is to maintain throughout the game the peak level of performance sought by the team. Look what Golden State has done with its bench. Al Attles, the Warrior coach, expertly shuffled his bench into the action and it proved successful because the reserves were ready both mentally and physically. There was no decline in performance when reserves went in.

The most frustrating positions are the last couple on a 12-man team. Those players rarely will play unless a key man is injured or ejected from a game. Still, they must stay in shape despite potential mental anguish.

Confidence is as essential to a player as his legs. Without it he is crippled. The bench can drain a man's confidence if he is not careful. If you find yourself on the tail end of a team and you wish to further your career, nurture that confidence. Take pride in your play during practice and in brief game appearances. Actually, much can be learned from the bench with a live laboratory in front of you, but you should realize that the only way to improve is to play.

Coming off the bench makes it difficult to learn from your mistakes. If you fear your coach will pull you after a mistake, it will inhibit your play, but nevertheless, it may be a situation you must learn to live with. Be patient and be ready when your chance—and everyone eventually gets a chance—arrives.

Whereas confidence is a mental condition, timing is physical and that, too, is difficult to maintain from the bench. Once your timing goes, the quality of your play disintegrates. You will discover that the moves you once made so gracefully have become cumbersome and awkward. During the season, when practices are sporadic and oftentimes brief, substitutes will find little time to keep their play sharp. To prevent their play from deteriorating, they have to work particularly hard in practice and possibly work out on their own.

If you find yourself on the bench, the only way you can expect to play more is to play well when the coach puts you in the game. You must realize he isn't keeping you on the bench because of a personality conflict. The coach is in charge and he has allocated playing time for various basketball reasons. It is your prerogative not to agree with him, and I am not sure you should if you want to be successful, but you must be patient to some degree.

Being sidelined is especially trying for a player accustomed to starting and playing a lot of minutes. It was a delicate transition for me when I joined the Lakers as a rookie after a successful college career at UCLA. I resented sitting on the bench. I thought I was a better player than I was and I still think so today. All players think they are better than they are. That's part of the make-up of a professional athlete.

Even as a substitute, you still are part of the team. Its welfare is your primary concern and you can help by accepting your role without bitterness and conflict. A morale problem can infect a team like a cancer, spreading its tentacles throughout. Teams don't need internal problems; it is difficult enough to win as it is.

POST-GAME

It would be ideal if after every game each player would say, "I played as well as I possibly could. I have no blame." Then each could forget about it, go his way, and get ready for the next.

If you lose and play poorly, however, don't dwell on it. It is finished and you can't bring the game back. There will be reasons, plenty of them, but just make mental notes. Don't tear yourself apart. When I was younger, I took defeats very hard, but I have mellowed over the years. What good can it possibly do to sit up all night replaying every move, trying to pinpoint the many blunders that turned the game into a defeat. It is the same after a win. Sure, you should be pleased, but not ecstatic. Just take it for what it is. One game out of 30, or 80 in the pros. Of course, if it is a championship game, then celebration is due.

After a game, I go over the stat sheet and study it for a few minutes. One tends to isolate the good things and dismiss the bad, but I make mental notes of errors (both of commission and of omission) so I can improve for the next game. There will always be things you can do a little better.

I generally take my time after a game. The first thing I do after leaving the locker room is to get something to eat. Usually I will have a big meal. Then I will relax. Sometimes it will take me a long time to unwind. Depending upon our schedule, I will either go out or return home or to my hotel room if there is another game the next night.

Each player has his own methods of relaxing after a game. Some will read, some will watch television, and some will just go to sleep. No matter what you do, don't dwell on the game. It only takes so long to analyze. Leave that to the coaching staff.

chapter three

team relationships

No matter at what level of basketball you are—high school, college, or professional—you will find the same basic conflicts, the same camaraderie, and usually the same buffoonery. You will find the coach at the front of the bus, along with the assistant, the trainer, and perhaps one or two of the more serious players. All the others will file in, moving to the rear, out of earshot.

Wherever you sit on the bus, however, you should remember that the most important factor in dealing with your coaching staff and teammates is respect. That there are diverse personalities on your team indicates it is a healthy one. You can't be best friends with everyone, but you can respect and expect it in return as a basketball player. Respect is the nucleus for all comfortable relationships. It opens lanes of communication as well as lanes on the fast break.

A team can have all the ingredients for success—a couple of tall and agile centers, strong sharpshooting forwards, and quick guards—but if the talents are not compatible, they will be wasted. There must exist a working rapport between players and between players and coaches.

Since the coach bears the responsibility of knitting a cohesive unit from a group of players, many of whom are temperamental and egotistical, his job is perilous. In this respect the basketball coach is unlike his equivalent in football, who is more akin to a general of an army. A basketball coach is a juggler, and the objects he juggles have personalities, feelings, and opinions.

THE COACH

The coach's ultimate goal is to coordinate his material so that 100 percent efficiency and ability can be realized from his team. He can't do it without the assistance and cooperation of the players, however. It must be a bilateral arrangement, with the coach's control established at the outset, whether it be at the beginning of the season or when a new player joins the club. All must comprehend the necessity of working together to enhance the possibilities of victory.

There will always be differences of opinion—and sometimes there should be—but one man in a group must assume the responsibility of leadership, and I believe the coach should be that man. A coach not in command of his players will have chaos. Conflicts, both personal and professional, will arise, spreading rapidly like a brush fire until all vestiges of team unity are in ruin.

Although it is unlikely in high school and rare in college, a power play occasionally will develop in the pros when the importance of a key player is placed over the coach by management. If the conflict between the two is irreconcilable and the player's vast influence is felt at the box office as well as on the court, management (or the athletic department at the college level) may believe it easier to replace the coach. It is a matter of control, and when it occurs it is obvious that the player holds the reigns.

I don't believe a player can make the decisions. He doesn't have the overall viewpoint or concern of the coach. The coach cares about

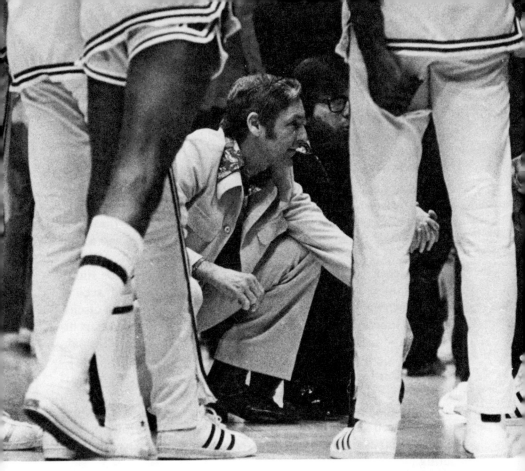

Laker coach Bill Sharman discusses strategy during a timeout.

the team, the performance, the organization, and the community, whereas the player generally is concerned about his particular situation within the framework of the team. As a rule, he thinks about himself, his career, and his game more often and more deeply than he does about the team and its welfare. Basketball is susceptible to this type of problem because of the limited numbers of players and the importance placed on the superstar. When management backs a player rather than a coach, it is not helping the team. Still, once such a situation arises, it is evident a new coach is needed because the old one lost the control required for the team to be effective.

To maintain control, the coach does not have to be a dictator. There is room on a basketball team for the interchange of ideas. Bill Sharman, one of the finest coaches in the game, always asks his players for suggestions. Of course, he doesn't always use them, but he does consider them, and the feedback he receives from his players helps him as a coach. He must do this delicately, however, for too much feedback can kindle confusion and eventually disaster.

The 1975 NBA championship series between Golden State and Washington provided a perfect example of what can happen when a coach throws out a problem to the team and receives too much discussion. Thanks to television, the public was allowed into the teams' huddles during timeouts. Golden State coach Al Attles had a firm hold on the Warriors, rapidly firing instructions, but on the Bullets' bench, coach K. C. Jones, his assistant, and several players simultaneously offered proposals, wasting valuable time and accomplishing nothing. There is a time and a place for widespread discussion, but a timeout isn't one of them. Then the coach must assert his authority and make decisions for the welfare of the team. The players must abide by those decisions, unflinchingly.

One reason for Sharman's willingness to accept ideas from his players is the caliber of talent he works with. Men like Jerry West, Wilt Chamberlain, Kareem Abdul-Jabbar, and myself were experienced and well versed in the game's tactics. Being a former player, Sharman realizes veteran players often have ideas worth considering.

Although coaches on other levels of the game may be less inclined to accept suggestions from players, they still must communicate. A player should know not only what to do but why to do it. Somehow, the coach must relate to his players that "this is the best way of doing it." If he has their respect, it will follow easily. This was one of John Wooden's greatest strengths. If you played for him there was no doubt you would play the game his way. He had an uncanny knack for relating to players. His extreme confidence was communicated effortlessly. His players believed if they did it the Wooden Way, the desired results would follow.

No one expects a coach to go through an entire season, or even a game for that matter, without making mistakes. However, if he makes glaring errors consistently, players may grow wary and varying degrees of strife may erupt. Once the coach loses the ability to make decisions, he begins to lose control of the team. Players won't always agree with the coach, but when his judgments begin to ham-

During a break in the action, I discuss strategy with Laker coach Bill Sharman.

per the team effort, a spokesman—perhaps the captain—should discuss the situation with him in behalf of the team. Naturally this problem will be much easier to handle if the coach is accessible.

Conversely, players should listen to the coach. He is the authority figure and it is assumed that just as a player applies himself totally to the benefit of the team, so does the coach.

Although the presumption that all players are treated equally is a tired cliché (which also happens to be unworkable), the coach should avoid holding grudges. He is dedicated to the team and its effort because that is his job. According to management, the coach is responsible for the team's performance. If it wins, he'll be congratulated; if it loses, he'll be criticized, perhaps even fired.

The player-coach relationship should be well defined. I believe the relationship is best when the coach is not too friendly with his players. Isolation is not necessary, but he should be somewhat aloof. After all, he will decide who will play and when. Sharman is like that and so are Red Holzman of New York and Dick Motta of Chicago. It is only natural that a coach have friendlier relations with some players than others, as is the case with Motta and Jerry Sloan. They communicate well and Sloan acts as a buffer between Motta and his teammates. Motta needs this sort of arrangement because he is more isolated from his players than most coaches.

If an individual feels he has been slighted by the coach, he has the right to clear the air. I have found it healthy to get the conflict off my chest. Let the coach know how you feel. He may not do anything about it, since more than likely he already has considered all options before making the decision that affected the disgruntled player. Most coaches will listen to a player's grievance. In this era of growing individual freedom, those who refuse are asking for trouble. Players respect a coach who will discuss problems frankly, particularly when the subject is playing time.

Don't let a coach ruin your appetite for basketball. Try to reconcile differences, but above all protect your career. If the impasse seems permanent, try to tolerate the situation for the length of the season or for the length of time you must play for the man. In the end, analyze and plot your career and, as a last resort, look to move on.

Chicago coach Dick Motta shouts instructions from the sidelines. In an era of freestyle basketball, he's been able to maintain a disciplined and controlled type of game with the Bulls.

In professional basketball you can request a trade, but not in college or high school. It would be somewhat ludicrous for a prep to go to his principal and ask to be traded to a high school across town where the coaching is more to his liking. In college, though, you can transfer. But you should carefully weigh all alternatives before making such a move. You must realize you will lose a year of eligibility, which can be vital to a young man polishing his skills. It depends on the circumstances. If you are an excellent player and hope to play professionally, remember that bad reputations linger. Many pro clubs won't touch a player with a history of what they call "attitude problems." Players have enough of a challenge with the game itself; they don't need that kind of label to overcome. Rather than rebelling, you may be better off gritting your teeth and playing through the difficulty. Just let it ride. Time does have a way of dissolving problems that seemed so dramatic six months earlier.

A high school coach may be reluctant to fully communicate with an athlete because of the age barrier. If you have difficulty with the coach on that level and have ambitions to play in college, you may find it necessary to work on your game by yourself. Being young, strong, and ambitious, a high school athlete should be able to circumvent clashes with the coach. Three or four years may seem like a long time, but chances are the problem, if one arises, won't surface until the junior or senior year. Even then, it probably is exaggerated. You honestly may feel you can't play for the coach, but you can if you put your future in the proper perspective.

As a rule there won't be any trouble with coaches. Be level-headed about your relationship, as both of you are trying to win. Listen to him attentively and follow his instructions. And if you have questions, ask. Make sure you understand what is expected of you. His primary function is to teach and yours to learn. It's simple, so keep it that way. Teaching remains important on all levels but is unfortunately neglected at times. A good coach will stress fundamental basketball because receptive players will always find something new to learn. Too many enter the pros today without a full command of the basics of the game. Their great physical ability has enabled them to get by without it. The summer is a good time to teach but few coaches do. They view their positions in the way most players do—as a six-month job. There is an old saying that basketball players are made in the summer and teams in the fall. That is particularly true in high school and college and should be, to a lesser extent, in the pros. Much can be done to improve a player's skills during the off-season.

COMMON DENOMINATOR: BASKETBALL

As a player, I've learned that I will not like all my teammates. It's human nature. Some will be good friends, some just friends, and others acquaintances. Hopefully, there will be no enemies. Players who congregate on a team past the high school level will have different backgrounds, personalities, and tastes. The one thing all have in common is basketball, and that is where respect should enter the relationships. Regardless of what your teammates do off the court, what they do on the court should be held in high esteem.

Basketball is a team game and everyone must work together in order to win. It is a form of communication that manifests itself through passes, screens, double teaming, and hopefully victory. You may not say two words to a teammate off court all season, but when he takes a couple of dribbles towards you, you had better know what is on his mind. If you had harsh words with a teammate moments before tipoff, don't allow that to prevent you from setting a pick for him. If your best friend is playing opposite you, stop him. Don't let him drive past you for an easy layin just because he's a nice guy. You are playing basketball, and personal grudges and friendships are immaterial. All that should matter on the court is your team and your role within it. Players will go their own ways after a game and it doesn't matter what they do. Nonetheless, the better teammates get along off court, the better they will play together.

Basketball players are creative by definition because their play—their individual art form—is impossible to duplicate. Thus, most are suspicious of criticism by their peers. Your role as a team member is to give help when asked; otherwise egos will clash and there is no telling what torrents will be unleashed. Criticism should be left to the coach; that's a headache he gets paid to deal with.

Whenever the subject of cliques arises, most coaches will tremble. They envision their team split asunder by jealousy, dissension, and

The Boston Five (from left to right), Cowens, White, Scott, Silas, and Havlicek, start up the court. Through the years the Celtics have best exemplified the spirit of team play.

discontent. I know cliques are small exclusive groups, but I don't believe they necessarily destroy a team. It seems that in every group, smaller groups will form. There always will be special relationships between a few who have interests in common. They will gravitate towards one another and there is no harm in that. What sometimes will happen, though, and what will worry the coach, is antagonism

among the groups—or cliques, if you prefer. You might have two or three players over here not communicating or openly hostile with two or three players over there. Then your team has trouble and those are the cliques that should be avoided. However, don't be alarmed if the fellows with whom you associate are not particularly friendly with another group or groups. There may even be some gossip, but usually it is harmless. Naturally, the buck gets passed when the team is losing.

Over the years, basketball has evolved into a game in which its parts are highly specialized. As a player, then, your job is defined and you should understand the responsibilities of the others. Although evaluating personnel is the duty of the coach, all players should realize the assets and liabilities of their teammates. If a player doesn't shoot well from 15 feet and beyond, the coach should make sure he doesn't shoot from there; but if you are a guard and you have noticed he has taken a few shots from outside his range, you might recommend that if he passes the ball backcourt and breaks to the basket he might get it right back for an easier shot. Instead of the 15-footer, he might get a seven-footer.

That is a more effective method of dealing with the situation than criticizing or resenting him for taking the bad shot. It isn't your obligation, but someone must make such suggestions when the coach isn't in position to take charge. Similar suggestions can be made when you have a good rapport with a teammate. Eventually you will learn who accepts constructive criticism and who doesn't.

Everyone, regardless of what field or business he is in, appreciates praise when it is due. So hand it out after a good play, a good shot, and especially after a good pass. Give him "five," or tell him, "good pass . . . nice shot . . . great play. . . ." Make sure he knows you recognized a play well done.

If you are a shooter, you will learn, if you haven't already, that passers are instrumental to your game. Wooden taught me the importance of complimenting a player who fed me a good pass. It enhances the chances of getting the good pass again. He won't force it if the opportunity doesn't exist, but he may become more aggressive in creating the situation.

Newspapers and fans, too, often ignore the passer and rebounder, but you can't. The morning paper after a game will glorify the scorer with a lengthy report of grace and daring, leaving just a sentence or two to wrap up the rebounds and assists. This is unfair, since all players make the team work, but it is the way the press and public choose to evaluate the game. A player, however, shouldn't be trapped by such analysis, for he knows the significance of all positions. Similarly, a scorer should take overblown accounts of his exploits in stride.

Scoring is the game's first attraction and just about every player, at some time in his career, is a scorer. A player may be primarily a rebounder, but remember he still likes to put the ball in the basket. If you are a guard you must know that. Try to set him up for a shot early in the game. Not only will he be appreciative, but he may be off to a hot night. He may score 15 or 20 points, rather than his usual eight or 10, in addition to his rebounding.

The team quarterback, as the leader, is responsible for maintaining the confidence of his teammates. During the course of a game, a player may go several minutes without touching the ball. The quarterback should be aware of what is happening on the floor and needs to get that particular player involved in the offense as soon as possible. If not, he should say so. Just tell the ball handler, "Come into the center," or "Let's go with the backdoor." That's one way of informing him he should be aware a player has been neglected the last four or five times down the floor.

A suggestion like that doesn't upset me. I figure it is a positive way of communicating and of keeping everyone involved in the play. When I'm not getting the ball, I tell the other guard. He understands.

From the guard position, you have a view of your offense. If you are bringing the ball down court on a three-on-two break, you have a choice, unless the defense is favoring one of the sides, of the player to whom to pass the ball. If Corky Calhoun and Cazzie Russell are on the wings, and the defense isn't overplaying Cazzie, I'll pass him the ball for the 15-foot jump shot. It's not that I hold a grudge against Corky, nor is it that I want to ignore him, it's just smart basketball. I would rather have Cazzie taking the shot and Corky, who is a better rebounder, going to the boards on the weak side.

Once again, you must know your teammates' capabilities. When a shooter like Brian Winters enters the game, it would be smart to get him a couple of quick shots to see if he hits them. He may be off to a good night. The same with Cazzie. They are explosive players who can get points in a hurry. The secret is to keep everyone involved; it isn't as easy as it looks, but it makes for a better and happier team.

Regarding players on other teams, there is no reason why you can't have friendly relationships. In fact, I think it sharpens the competitive edge. I found it to be true playing against former college teammates like Mahdi Abdul-Rahman (Walt Hazzard) and Keith Erickson. You always try to hold your own against your friends, and I believe it to be a healthy climate. Cliff Hagen and Frank Ramsey, who were teammates at Kentucky, had a similar relationship when they were in the pros. Personal pride and respect seem to be accentuated when your opponent is a friend or former teammate.

The one thing that keeps everything in order on a team is victory. When you win consistently, everyone is happy and everyone gets a share of the praise. A few years ago when the Lakers won 33 straight games, all contributed and whatever potential problems existed never surfaced. Jealousies always will be present to some degree, but if a team is winning and the players are being utilized properly, they won't erupt. After all, how can one complain when the ultimate goal of winning is being realized?

Good relationships are extremely important, yet difficult to achieve because of the many human factors involved. As an individual, you can do your part by fostering friendships with your teammates. Be yourself and try not to inhibit the others.

THE LEADER

Being selected team captain is an honor, but his importance diminishes in the higher levels of the game. The position really means little in the professional game. The captain meets with the officials and the opponent's captain before the game for a perfunctory ceremony in which everyone shakes hands and very little is said. In the beginning of a season, there may be some discussion if a new rule was introduced that requires an explanation. Usually, you just shake hands and return to your team and await the start of the game.

The important individual on the team actually is the team or floor leader. Your leader should be one of the better players. He should be respected for his ability, able to communicate with and understand the problems of the players, and judicious enough to act capably as a buffer between the players and coach. Experience also is a vital

Wilt Chamberlain demonstrates his dominance and strength as he dunks the ball. He was an unquestioned leader on and off the court.

factor, considering that much of his leadership will be tested under stress.

The Lakers haven't had an election of a team captain since I have been with the club. Wilt Chamberlain was picked by Sharman, and when he left Jerry West was selected. Then it passed to me after West retired.

I'm not sure that appointing a leader is the best method. You can't say, "Gail's going to be the leader." Becoming a leader is a subliminal process in which a player emerges into the role. It takes time and the development of character. You will find that, as a season progresses, players will begin to seek out one of their teammates in critical situations. He's the one who should be your leader and captain.

A guard often is the leader because he handles the ball and initiates the plays. Chamberlain, of course, wasn't a guard, yet he was a

leading and powerful force when he was in the league. When Wilt spoke, you listened. It was simple. You respected him for a variety of reasons, primarily because he was a great player, but also because of his physical stature and dominating personality. You wouldn't always agree with everything he said—at least I didn't—but there was no disputing the fact that he was the leader. Same with West, no one questioned his leadership. Both were examples of the prototype team captain and floor leader. They had many years of experience and the respect of all the players on their teams as well as in the entire league.

Off the court, the team leader should remain one of the players. He is not an assistant coach, nor is he a part of management. Preferably, he will be a gregarious individual who can easily communicate with everybody. But he can get by as a recluse. After all, the critical part of his position is on the court. Wilt was a loner, Jerry only associated with a few, and I guess I keep pretty much to myself, too. So, I'm not sure he has a definitive role off the court. Surely, good relations will carry over onto the floor, but a leader will win his position by what he does with the basketball and not with his mouth.

THE MEDIA

Since basketball is dependent upon the fan, it also is subject to the whims of the media, which acts as an intermediary. Its job is to inform the public; but a problem arises, I believe, when those in the media have little knowledge of the game and their reports are either inaccurate or spotted with half-truths. Naturally, there are exceptions.

Since I have been misquoted at times, and have read reports the day after a game that bore no resemblance to what occurred on the floor, I am wary of the press. I have had some bad press that I thought was undeserved, but perhaps it was my fault for not speaking up. Still, so much of the relationship seems to be talk just for the

Bill Walton (right) tries to stop Lucius Allen's baby hook. Walton, I believe, will be a dominating force and leader for Portland in the future.

sake of talking—which is a charade in which I don't believe. Maybe it is a con game, I don't know.

I am a private person with a tendency to remain silent unless pressed for answers. I admit I'm suspicious, but I'm trying to improve my image, for I have come to realize reporters are merely doing their job and they must have opinions and ideas from the players for their stories.

The press will continue to exist and it is smart for a player to accept it and be accessible to it. In the past decade, a loud outcry has been made by members of the Los Angeles media over UCLA's policy of barring the press from its players. It started when Kareem Abdul-Jabbar entered the school in 1965 and carried through the Bill Walton years. Diverse reasons were given for the policy, which resulted in an emotional stagnation of the key figures it was designed to protect—Abdul-Jabbar and Walton.

Abdul-Jabbar, who since has improved his relations with the press, recently said that the press ban impeded his growth as a man and that he could have handled the inquiries even though he consented to the policy. The adversary relationship a player has with the media is a potentially healthy one and should not be avoided, although at times it is tempting to do so.

It still bothers me that few reporters possess a working knowledge of the game, but that must be overlooked when considering the fact that the press can provide an enormous boost to a player's career. Those with excellent press have received publicity and exposure, which have helped them financially and made them popular among the fans.

THE FANS

Fans will love you, praise you, ignore you, boo you, and hate you. Just accept it for what it is, for in the end it will be the performance they respect. The easiest way to be well received is to play good basketball, since that is what they are looking for.

To some fans you will be an object for releasing frustrations and anxieties they have built up during the day. As an athlete and entertainer, you must accept that, so long as they don't threaten bodily

Here I sign autographs for a group of kids following a Laker game.

harm. Don't antagonize them, for that will only incite them more. Angry fans can inhibit your game if you let them.

Considering that fans perpetuate the game, the player has two major obligations: to play as well as he can and to make himself available on occasion as a public figure, which includes the signing of autographs.

Autographs can be a monumental hassle. Picture yourself leaving an arena after a hard, rugged game: awaiting you are your bus, which will take you to the airport for a midnight flight, and perhaps 100 youngsters waving pencils and paper in your face.

What do I do?

I keep moving! But while making my way to the bus, I sign as many autographs as I can. I try to be human about the thing. I sign the autographs because, in essence, I am satisfying a desire of the fan, but I can't stand there all night; I also have commitments to my team, which is waiting, and my family, which is waiting for me after a home game.

I can't make all the fans happy. If I sign autographs for a few, the others will be angry. They will yell, sometimes obscenely, and generally harass me. Really, the verbal barrage that players are subject to under these circumstances is unfair. Some fans refuse to understand commitments.

When I can't sign all the autographs, I often ask them to write me care of the Forum in Inglewood and I'll send them an autographed picture, but that will not satisfy those who want it now. All you can do is bear with them.

As a rule, players should be proud to sign autographs and answer fan mail. It is an indication of their success and acceptance by the fans. Although it loses its luster after a while, you shouldn't lose sight of your obligation.

The athlete is part of the input in society, not only for children, but for others as well. Kids will remember the things you do and for the moment you are with them, your presence will make a significant impact. If you refuse to sign autographs or otherwise live up to your public obligations, you may leave a bad taste, which will linger for years. When you sign an autograph you make someone happy, and I think that's a pretty nice position to be in.

THE OFFICIALS

There are two things to remember about the referees: one, they are human; and two, they are part of the game and belong on the court.

They will make mistakes and, more than likely, they will make plenty. But that is the nature of the game. The players are big and the

I question a call made by former NBA official Jack Madden. I lost the argument, as usual.

play is fast, making it almost impossible for the officials to make all the correct calls. You must learn to accept their mistakes. Arguing will only get you a technical foul or two and ejection from the game. You won't change the call, that's for sure.

There are times you can discuss a call with an official, but don't embarrass him. Remember to delete the expletives, though, because there are a few magic words that automatically warrant a technical.

I try to say a word or two at the foul line or during a timeout. Some referees won't talk to you, which is irritating because they should leave room for interpretation and communication. They shouldn't isolate themselves, but they shouldn't be subjected to abuse, either. It doesn't help the game when coaches and players are ejected.

Pro basketball would eliminate many of the tirades if it levied a heavier fine for technical fouls. I don't think a coach should ever be kicked out of a game. His job is to direct the team and without him it loses its leadership, robbing the fans of the quality performance they paid to see, when he is thrown out. A large fine, however, will put a halt to some of their infantile harangues.

It has just been in the last few years that I have realized how futile it is to argue with the referees. I have gone from 15 technicals one season to none or just a few. They are out there to call the game as they see it. They're honest. I don't think there are any who aren't. Sure, you may see a call differently, but you may have seen the play from a different angle, perhaps a poorer one. If you continue to abuse an official, it's like anything else, animosity will build and he may start looking for you to foul. They won't admit to that, but it happens.

Generally, officials don't influence the outcome of a game. Those who blame a loss on a call are looking for excuses. If you shoot better, defend better, rebound better, you will win regardless of the fouls that officials call. There will be violations that hurt you because they occurred at critical times, but if you had played better basketball prior to the calls, they wouldn't be that important. Considering the pace of the game, I truly believe they do a remarkable job.

However, I would like to see three officials used in all games. An extra pair of eyes would clean up the hands and much of the contact, which has taken a lot of the finesse out of the game. Basketball is a game of finesse, speed, and quickness, and those elements are disappearing because of the rough play.

One argument against a third referee, which I believe to be wrong, is that he will increase the number of fouls. Nobody wants a parade to the foul line. There may be more violations called at first, but eventually the players will adapt their play and the fouls will level off.

The league often has experimented with the third ref, but it tempers his power. He is used to call just the noncontact fouls, like three seconds in the key, goal tending, five seconds to put the ball in bounds, and the like. If you're going to give him a whistle, I think he should be able to use it whenever he spots a violation.

Basketball has grown a great deal in the past quarter century. The players are better, the rules have changed, and the action is faster; yet the manpower for controlling the game has remained the same. The time has arrived for a third official and I believe it will make the game even better than it is.

chapter four

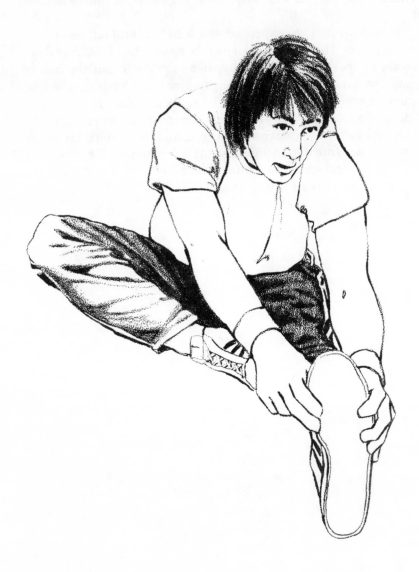

training

Training is the back alley of sports. For all the hours spent on stage, the athlete spends many more sweating in gymnasiums, on tracks, and on fields beyond the critical eye of the public. It sometimes is tedious; it is difficult; it can be painful; but, above all, it is necessary. Training is a sacrifice all athletes must make for their sport, particularly for basketball, which is physical and fast-paced.

The purpose of training is to give the individual maximum performance with minimum wear and tear. Theoretically, a basketball player should suffer only accidental injuries. Muscle pulls—painful and lingering injuries, which occur more frequently in basketball than in other sports—perhaps can be avoided (at least the frequency can be reduced) by dedicated, year-round training.

There are so many different theories of how an athlete should train that it would be impractical to advance them all here. I'm not sure there is one right way, but there have been things that have helped me to achieve the success I have had.

OFF-SEASON

Most athletes have a great deal of God-given ability, which is easy to take for granted. The athlete is young and his body can do marvelous things, which seemingly never will end. Once the season ends he can hang up his sneakers, letting the dust accumulate until he has to resurrect them six months later when the summer months are gone. During the off-season there is no one to push him, no one but himself. You will find, however, that most pro athletes keep active during the off-season.

You are an athlete 12 months a year. You must maintain a level of conditioning that will allow you to regain peak form through a few weeks of hard workouts. You can do this by participating in other sports, by running, by playing basketball, or by devising a formal program—which may or may not include weight training. Sports I have found helpful for basketball players are tennis, volleyball, and racquetball. Each requires quick movements and footwork similar to those used on the basketball court.

Players sometimes are discouraged from working out with weights because long sinewy muscles are needed in basketball, not bulging ones. Nevertheless, last summer I trained with weights twice weekly using the Nautilus weight machines. It is a total body-conditioning program, which uses weights for variable resistance. It is not a body-building program. There are approximately 20 exercises. Each muscle, beginning with the largest ones in the back and stomach, is exercised in proper sequence. The idea is to balance all the muscles so all are equally strong.

The program is new to me, yet the results have been good. I believe it has helped my game. It has increased my overall strength,

(Facing page.) Off-season training has become important to me, particularly as I get older. Here I'm working out on two of the Nautilus weight machines.

stamina (which is important over a long season), and mental toughness. The program was designed to prolong my career and I believe I have taken a step in that direction.

A weight-training program may not appeal to everyone, but every player should do something. If you're young, you may decide to play basketball all the time. That's fine, but eventually you may want to increase your strength. Weights will do that and so will running, which also will improve your quickness and stamina.

The last five years, I have participated in a running program directed by Jim Bush, the UCLA track coach. It has made my legs much stronger and I have found that when I need quick movements and a burst of speed over a short distance, I am able to achieve the maximum quickness I have. To achieve your maximum quickness, you need what Bush calls a "strong base," which can be acquired through running distances and building up your legs and wind.

You should begin your running program at least 10 to 12 weeks before training camp opens so that you have the strong base when you begin playing. You start by running distances. I start with one mile a day and eventually work up to 3½ miles. Once I've achieved my strong base, I begin my hill work. I repeatedly sprint up the hill adjacent to the UCLA campus that is approximately a quarter-mile long.

When I was growing up, basketball season was comparatively short (the high school season lasted from the end of October until the middle of January), so in the spring I played other sports, particularly baseball. It is good for kids to be exposed to a variety of athletics. Now, however, if you plan to be a basketball player, be prepared for a full-time sport. High school players in the larger cities have well-organized summer leagues where the competition is keen and the level of ability high. If you want to improve, you should join. Some players play 10 to 12 months out of the year and it only figures they will be a little better in the long run than those who play just a few months.

Off-season training is in the hands of the individual. A player can choose to further develop his skills, condition his body, or do nothing. The dedicated athlete, the one who wants to improve, will train.

PRESEASON

By the time your team congregates in the fall for practice or pre-season, you should be in good condition and ready to play. You don't necessarily have to be at peak condition, but you should be able to take the rigors of two-a-day workouts, wind sprints, and the like. In addition, be prepared for the mental burden created by the fierce battles for position.

One of John Wooden's pet phrases was, "You play like you practice." Many players don't agree with him, but most coaches do. I have found it to be generally true. If you have a good preseason, chances are you will have a good season, too. At the very least, you will get off to a good start with a confident and positive outlook. On the contrary, a player who loafs will find it difficult to catch up and may soon discover others playing ahead of him who should not be.

The coach's primary task, especially in college and high school, is to study the talent he has and determine what system and which players are best. He will spend much of the preseason figuring out the details. He always is evaluating his personnel, during summer leagues and even while watching three-on-three games, but he is more intent when he has his players together during this critical period. In practice you must show him what you can do, that you can handle the pressure and the play in game situations. He will notice everything you do on the floor. If you have improved vastly since the previous season, or you are playing for the coach for the first time, this is your chance to prove to him you can play.

One who plans to make a career of basketball should learn to like practice, because it never ends. I'm 32 and have been practicing basketball every fall afternoon for almost 20 years. The routine and repetition remain the same. You should be prepared to work hard and put forth a maximum effort if you are to play once the season begins. During the last four or five years, I have found I have my best seasons when I report to training camp in good shape with my weight down and my legs strong because of the running program.

You have to discipline yourself. Practices are long and hard and you must continually push yourself if you are to be in peak form for the start of the season. Mental toughness isn't merely coming

through in pressure situations for your club, it also is the running, the drills, and the contact. Nothing comes easy.

Times will arise when you can pace or coast through some of the drills. But the only person you are hurting is yourself. Over the course of the season, those extra free throws or that extra step of hustling back on defense can help your team. When Pete Newell, general manager of the Los Angeles Lakers, was the coach at the University of California, Berkeley, he would put his players through the defensive sliding drills for 20 minutes at a time. His drills are legend. If you have ever done them, even for just a few minutes, you know how excruciating the pain can be. You have to pay the price to be a winner and Newell's teams always were known for their tenacious defense.

Don't worry about getting tired. Everyone does. In fact, when I was at UCLA I would get so exhausted after a workout I would have to go to my room and lie down for a few hours. That proved to me that I got something out of the practice. If you really work hard and push yourself, you should be tired when it is over. Then you have time to rest and relax.

Once preseason practice begins, you will have a limited time, perhaps one month, before the season is underway. During that period you will spend much of the time working on the fundamentals—the same fundamentals you worked on the year before and the year before that. Even in the pros, the same basic drills used in high school are repeated daily. High school coaches may teach more and spend more time on the fundamentals, but throughout your career you will discover the emphasis always is placed there.

On the Lakers, we have two-a-day workouts every day possible. Coach Sharman covers fundamentals and plays in the morning and conditioning in the afternoon. His workouts are well-planned and rigorous. I don't know how hard the Boston Celtics of the 1950s worked, but if that is where Sharman learned his conditioning methods, they must have been tough. He believes in hard work. I have heard stories that when he was a player, he would practice on

(Facing page.) Running, which is somewhat boring at times, also is part of my off-season training. As a part of my program, I run the UCLA stadium steps.

his own—after the team workout. He is dedicated and it has paid off for him, both as a player and as a coach.

Most players think training is drudgery, which it can be, but it can also be fun. The sacrifice and the discipline don't necessarily take the fun out of the game. In fact, if you have a positive attitude it will be easy. There will be things you will not want to do. I don't particularly enjoy weight training and I don't like to run just for the sake of running, but I do it because I know it will help me as a basketball player, and nothing is more important to me. Running is boring, but I try to think about the fun I have playing basketball, and that keeps me going.

SEASON

Once the season begins, the length of practice winds down. Still, you must manage to maintain your peak condition, your self-discipline, and your game.

The professional season is much different from the high school and college ones. We play so many more games that conditioning is less of a factor than fatigue, particularly for the starters. We sometimes play four times a week, and those who play 35 to 45 minutes a game must pace themselves if they are to remain effective. If I have a tough game one night, I won't run hard in practice the next day. Of course, I will go through the drills, the half-court scrimmages, and whatever else the coach has scheduled, but I won't go full-tilt.

Primarily I will work on my technique, timing, and defense. With shorter and less frequent practice sessions, you and your coach should be concerned with quality workouts. Oftentimes I arrive at practice a half hour early and just concentrate on my shooting, paying particular attention to such fine points as follow-through and body balance. All it is is a tune-up. You try to keep your shot, or whatever other part of your game you're working on, well-oiled. If done properly, you will have sufficiently practiced your shooting before your team's workout even begins.

Jerry West also conscientiously strived for quality workouts. He would get to the gym early and just concentrate on his shooting. He wouldn't talk to anybody and he wouldn't fool around. He would

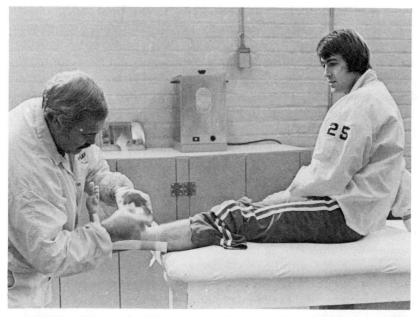

Taping is a part of my daily ritual. Laker trainer Del Tanner tapes my ankle before a practice.

shoot jump shots standing still, off the dribble, going to his right, and going to his left. He would shoot from all over the floor. Once the actual practice session began, he wouldn't even shoot. Instead, he would concentrate on other phases of the game, like passing, dribbling, and defense. He didn't work out long. He didn't have to because he was playing all the time and he was in shape. All he needed was a tune-up to sharpen his timing.

Many players never understood what West was doing. Most just go out and play. They don't realize they should compartmentalize their game. West did and so do I. You break down the many facets and work on each one individually. It's like taking apart an engine of a car, cleaning it up, and putting it back together again. It really makes sense. You already know and understand how all the parts work together to form a unit, but for that unit to be working smoothly, each piece must be functioning properly.

I realize it is somewhat different in high school and college. There you usually play only on weekends, so you continue to scrimmage during the week. John Wooden had his teams practice fundamental drills every day. He also would have several dummy scrimmages planned. For example, he would have his first string concentrate on defense at one end of the court and when it gained possession of the ball it used the fast break to get down to its offensive end. Then he would stop play and have the first string set up on defense again. In effect, he was compartmentalizing the game into team defense and the fast break.

You can always improve your game, even during the season. Competition gets better every year, so you must keep up with it. Look for new moves and polish your old ones. Work harder on defense, timing, body balance, and jumping. Great players like Elgin Baylor and Julius Erving have proved a player can do almost anything imaginable with his body on the basketball floor.

Substitutes don't play as much as the others, so the conditioning factor becomes vital to their development. Somehow you must stay in shape. Your timing can vanish in a week or two if you are not careful. The substitute must be aware of his situation. Not only must he improve his techniques like the starters, but he must find a way and the time to keep his conditioning and his timing sharp.

DIET AND WEIGHT

As any woman will tell you, there are a variety of diets in circulation. Which one do you pick? I don't know. The important thing is that you eat healthy foods and that the diet is balanced. If you are young and not inclined to put on excessive weight, I don't think you need a structured diet.

It is important for an athlete to watch his weight, both during the season and during the off-season. When you gain a lot of weight, you will lose your body balance and quickness and it will put stress on joints not used to it, making them susceptible to injury.

Many athletes have a tendency to put on weight after a season. They will eat the same amount of food, but they won't be burning up as many calories. I'm conscious of keeping my weight down all year.

I figure I'm a pretty good player at 175 pounds, but at 180 I begin to lose the quickness that is so vital to my game. Quickness is important to everyone's game, but even more so to the little man's. He doesn't have the strength to fall back on. A forward, center, or big guard can get away with a few extra pounds. Quickness really is the only physical advantage I have. So added weight can create a few problems for me.

Many people think weight and strength are synonymous, but they're not. You should play as light as you can, particularly when you get older and your metabolism rate begins to slow down. Be careful about playing too light, however, because you reach a point where you begin to lose some strength.

Coach Sharman and I often have discussed my weight and the weight of basketball players in general. He, too, believes a player should play as light as possible, but not to the point where it affects his strength. A player needs plenty of strength to play four times a week, or twice in two or three days. Recovery time is very important. A player must have the strength to come back the next night after a game.

Injuries can ruin your weight. You're playing light, you're burning up all the calories you're eating, and Wham!—you get hurt. You continue to eat the same amount, but you're no longer burning it up. If you're not careful, you will gain weight, which will slow your return to the team. Consequently, you might have to change your diet when injured.

All athletes have different eating habits and their stomachs react differently to different kinds of foods. During the season, as I explained earlier, it is best to eat carbohydrates for pregame meals because they provide instant energy for a game. Otherwise, you want to keep fattening foods at a minimum. I doubt if people ever will agree on what constitutes a balanced diet. Generally, it includes foods that keep your weight at a stable level over a prolonged period of time. The so-called balanced diet is always a good idea.

INJURIES

All players realize that injuries sometimes may occur, but they can

Before every practice, I loosen up with stretching exercises. I
believe these exercises reduce the chances of pulled muscles.

minimize the problem by taking proper precautions, which will reduce their frequency, taking care of them immediately and properly when they occur, and taking a positive mental outlook during rehabilitation.

The most effective method for preventing injuries is to be in the best possible physical condition. Many players have had their careers cut short because of nagging injuries, which ultimately dimmed their mental approach to the game. And many times the injury, such as a pulled muscle, which may seem somewhat harmless, was a result of not being in shape.

This happened to Jerry West. He could still be playing today, but he pulled muscles in his stomach and was troubled the entire 1973-74 season. He was in and out of the lineup and when he was able to play he figured he couldn't meet the high standards he always had set for himself. It affected him mentally and subsequently led to his retirement.

Stretching exercises are preventive medicine. I do a number of them every day to keep my muscles limber and loose. I believe they reduce the chances of pulling muscles. To honestly stretch a muscle, you must get into the right position and concentrate. Stretching exercises are like yoga exercises. Muscles don't stretch like rubber bands, they come uncoiled. To do this, you must remain in a static position for approximately 50 seconds. A complete stretching program will take about 20 minutes and should be done every day, even during the off-season.

Some muscles are overdeveloped and some underdeveloped, so it is important to balance them. In basketball players, usually the leg muscles are overdeveloped and the stomach and hamstring muscles are underdeveloped. The Nautilus weight program mentioned earlier is designed to balance and strengthen all the muscles.

Sprained ankles are common injuries in basketball. Most players, at one time or another in their careers, have experienced them. If you are unfortunate enough to sprain an ankle, the first thing is to apply ice to reduce the swelling. Then have X-rays taken as a precautionary measure. It is important that when you are injured, you seek competent medical help and listen to and heed the doctor's advice. He knows more about athletic injuries than you do and

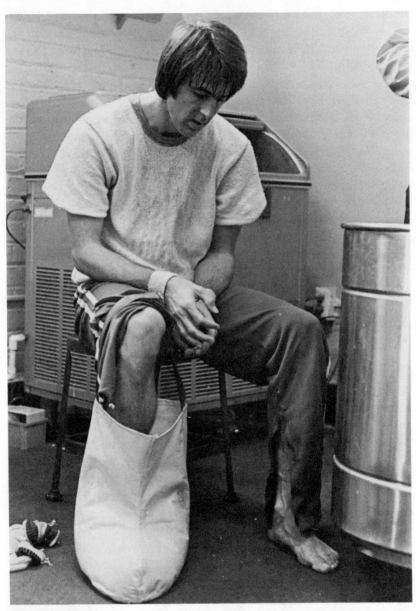

Sprained ankles have occurred to me frequently during my career. Immediate treatment requires the soaking of my foot in ice.

wants you back on the floor as soon as possible, but not so soon that further damage might occur.

If your injury is of a serious nature, like torn knee ligaments, much of your recovery will depend upon how well you respond to rehabilitation. Rehabilitation is difficult because it is like training all over again. You must be patient and follow the schedule the therapist has devised. Rushing it may compound the injury.

Whenever you are injured, psychologically you become very depressed, because you simply can't do what you were doing before. You feel helpless and melancholy. I experienced that several years ago when I severely sprained an ankle. I didn't do much but sit around all day. I'd go to a game and sit on the sidelines and hobble along on crutches. I wasn't used to it.

Whenever possible, depending upon the nature of the injury, try to keep your physical conditioning at its normal level. Of course, the extent of the injury will determine what exercises you can do. With an ankle injury, it may be difficult to run, but you can do other things to keep in condition. Also, consult a doctor or trainer about maintaining your cardiovascular level.

The object of rehabilitation is to enable the athlete to be physically and mentally in shape when he returns to the team. It is the trainer's responsibility to put the athlete on a total program, one that will maintain the peak condition he had achieved before the injury. The athlete must always cooperate. He must have a tremendous desire to return to action as quickly as possible.

Your body is your bread and butter, so take care of it. If you train and eat properly, you will get more out of it and enhance the possibility of prolonging your career.

chapter five

basketball as a career

On buses on the way to hotels, arenas, and airports, I sometimes stare vacantly out the window at numerous unknown faces who are fighting city rush-hour traffic making their way home after a mundane workday and reflect upon my career as a basketball player.

What would I do if I couldn't shoot a jump shot?

I've thought about it many times and, truthfully, I don't know. In college, I took business courses, but I'm not qualified to be an accountant, a marketing specialist, or a real estate broker.

For as long as I can remember, I played basketball and I never seriously considered doing anything else. In a way, if you discount summer employment while a student, I have never held a job. If someone asks me what I do for a living, I say I play basketball. But that's not a job. It's play, just as it was years ago when I would go to

John Wooden, former UCLA basketball coach, gives encouragement to his players. He, my father, and my high school coach, Nelson Burton, have been the most instrumental figures in my basketball career.

the gym, basketball in hand, and take winners in a three-on-three pickup game.

And then I'll take a closer look at one of those cars driving by. In it sits a man, his brow lined, his eyes reddened, and his mind intent on matters far more serious than the world of games. He has a job and his existence revolves around it. He probably is secure in his regular paychecks (and what they have purchased over the years) and is permitted two, maybe three, weeks of frolic for an annual vacation. He also has his dreams of what could have been.

A basketball player, by contrast, actually lives his dreams, and for that I am thankful. The rewards are great, but like everything else, there are disadvantages, especially when you consider that an athlete's career usually ends in his thirties.

"I WANT TO BE A PRO"

Over the years, many rewards have come to me because of basket-

I'm scrambling for a loose ball as a college player at UCLA. I wore No. 25 even then.

ball. I am successful financially, I have enjoyed a lot of publicity, I have had doors opened to me that normally wouldn't have, and I am proud to be at the top of my profession. More important, I am doing something I love to do. All else pales in comparison.

Ideally, I would think, everyone's goal is to achieve happiness and, as most adults will attest, money and fame don't guarantee it. You may note that the people who are truly successful are the ones who are happy with what they are doing. Unfortunately, few ever are. Basketball players, however, fall into that rare category of people who earn their living through their own creative talents. In that respect, we are artists.

I know I am lucky. But becoming a professional basketball player is not a result of some grand design I devised when I was a child. It just happened. I was attracted to the game as a young boy, I played a lot, and I improved a lot. One step followed the other. I was a star in high school and was offered a college scholarship. Then I was a star in college and was drafted by the pros. It sounds so simple and in many ways it was. Looking back, I would say the most important attribute a basketball player has is his heart for the game.

Many kids play basketball. Most love the game. Those who don't will play for a while and eventually grow tired and bored. The youngster who gets beat time and again will eventually wonder what he is doing playing basketball. He'll quit and find another interest. There's nothing wrong with that. Basketball isn't the end result; it's not the main thing in life. If you don't love the game and you won't devote the time it takes to become really good, then you should pursue something else. But if you do love it and are successful, you will benefit from the thrill of winning, the cheers, and the pride that accompanies the fulfillment of your ability.

Once you have reached that point, you become dedicated and your dreams become goals. How many times have you heard a boy say, "I want to be a pro!" But that is not reality. Somewhere along the line, and it is impossible to determine exactly where, you may discover that there is a chance. You begin to set your goals: a prep star, a college scholarship, an All-American, a pro. As the competition and your ability improve, the goal comes into focus. You have had some success and, before you know it, you're a professional.

I'm driving to the basket against the big man, an ability that always has been part of my game.

You are among a select group of people whose job it is to play.

There are many outlets for a youth's almost boundless energy: music, art, reading, science, and many forms of athletics. If you really enjoy playing basketball, you don't consider the financial rewards, the headlines, or the notoriety. All that accompanies success, but they don't exist initially. The real rewards, which always are present, are intangible—happiness and satisfaction. They keep a youngster playing into the night. When he comes home, his mother wants to know where he has been all day and why he is late for dinner. The answer . . . basketball. All great players in their youth have come home to cold dinners and irate parents. They have stayed at the gym for that extra hour or two, trying to win just a couple more games. The more you play, the better you become.

The 1964 NCAA champion UCLA Bruins were successful because we played together as a team. Here I went up for a jump shot on the fast break but spotted and passed to Jack Hirsch, who had a better shot than I did. Two other prominent professional players are Keith Erickson, No. 53, and Paul Silas, then of Creighton University, at right.

I've always believed if you're going to do something, try to be the best. Do it right. And if you reach the pinnacle of your profession, you can be proud of a job well done. As an athlete, you're constantly striving to be the best. That's what competition breeds and I believe it is healthy and invigorating. The closer you come to the top, the greater will be the respect you will receive from the public and your peers. The way mass communications are today, a player considered one of the best in his sport is a national celebrity, a folk hero of sorts.

As Bill Russell once noted, athletes in this country are treated like royalty. Many people are frustrated athletes and have great admiration for those who have achieved success in athletics. That's very characteristic of the United States, I believe, and of other countries as well. It is a condition that has evolved, and to an athlete it is flattering. It's nice to be known and recognized, although at times it is difficult to handle when the fame comes suddenly and swiftly.

Being a celebrity does have its inconveniences. Your privacy will be invaded and your individuality will come under microscopic scrutiny by the press and public.

A lot of people enjoy their privacy and athletes are no exception. During the season, I spend a great deal of time playing basketball and when I come home I like to rest and relax with my family. Often, however, I'm prevented because of demands on my time made by the media, requests for appearances, various charity functions, and the like. I don't want to upset or offend anyone, but it is physically impossible for me to do everything that people ask. So, I have learned I sometimes must say no.

If you compare the family life of a basketball player to that of the norm, I guess ours would be considered unusual because of the long season and the many hours spent on the road—a sometimes torturous, never-ending series of gaseous buses, stuffy airplanes, bustling hotel lobbies, and pungent locker rooms. There have been so many upheavals in our society in recent years that I'm not sure that a norm exists any longer. Sure, many people still work from nine to five and come home after work to spend the evening with their families, but now women are working more and practically everyone's family life is changed to some degree.

The lifestyle of a professional athlete is different. We have no regular hours, there are no clocks to punch, and our work takes us from one end of the country to the other. I may be on the road for five days and then come home for five. It is a lifestyle my family and I have grown accustomed to. My wife and I have known about the travel for as long as we have been together and we have adjusted accordingly. Others probably would find the schedule difficult, as I would find it difficult working from nine to five. It's not bizarre, nor is it a drudgery, although it may appear that way to someone who has never experienced it.

I'm guarding Michigan All-American Cazzie Russell, who later was to become a teammate of mine on the Lakers, in the 1965 NCAA championship game—which we won.

As in other professions, the game is conducive to the making of lasting, sincere friendships. Inevitably, you will become attached to the other players because of kindred interests and experiences. Once the game is underway, of course, friendships shouldn't interfere with your play. But off court the rapport among players usually is warm. All of your peers have had many of the same experiences to get where all of you are. You may have been raised in different environments, but everyone has respect for others who do the same things well.

Basketball players are treated well, meet many interesting people, live comfortably, have a considerable amount of free time, and are exposed to numerous adventures and challenges because of their role in society. It is a wonderful way to make a living, primarily because a dream you once had has become real.

THE END COMES EARLY

One of the disappointments inherent in basketball comes for those who don't make it. It is a sobering time in one's life. It is unfortunate, but it is a situation that can happen to anybody, in any field. What about the man who goes to law school and can't pass the state bar examination? Or, what happens if he passes the bar only to discover he can't cope with the courtroom, or he makes a few blunders, which stifle his career? He spent many years studying and working to be an attorney, yet for one reason or another it doesn't work out the way he had hoped. We're all faced with such complications. As you grow older, you must learn to cope with reality.

There are many boys who love the game and want to be professionals, but their abilities will only take them so far. When your time as a player runs out, an adjustment, which becomes more major the more deeply you become involved in the sport, is required. It should only hurt a youngster a short while. He'll find other interests almost immediately. A player cut from his college team will suffer as long as it takes his ego to recover, but the professional will despair the most. The damage to his ego will be exceeded only by that to his pocketbook. Every player's time eventually runs out. When a professional nears the end of his career and notices that younger players are doing

things he used to be able to do with ease, he too, must face reality.

Someday it happens, and it can happen at the age of 18, when you are just entering college, or at 35, after a long career as a professional. It can be tough, but you must separate your dreams from your reality. If you are not equipped to be a basketball player, then accept it and move on.

It's the nature of the game that an athlete will reach his peak early in life. The fame, the fortune, and the public exposure he has achieved through basketball may never be achieved again. In other fields, a successful man may not reach his peak until his fifties or sixties, but in basketball it will come in one's late twenties or early thirties. The glory he has at that age may be gone forever, and it can be a depressing reality for him to accept. You can imagine what it's like, thinking that you have over half your life to live and it is all downhill.

Of course, it doesn't have to be approached in that way, but some athletes do approach it in that way. A player must remember that retirement is inevitable and when it arrives it should be confronted graciously. It will compel a major decision, which will affect his future. He shouldn't spend all his time worrying about it; he should just remember to prepare as it approaches.

There are times in everyone's life when adversities must be accepted and dealt with. You have to sit down and say, "This has happened, now where do I go from here?" That's tough sometimes.

I don't want to discourage boys from playing the game by telling them someday it will end. When I was young, I didn't think about it. It was the furthest thing from my mind. I played because it was fun. I never knew how far I would get with basketball and, what's more, I didn't care. Maybe I'll get tired of the game in a few more years. Then it will be easy, I'll just walk away.

Throughout my career, there have been several turning points, but the moments I remember with the most fondness are the championships. I have been fortunate to win on every organized level: high school, college, and professional. Those seasons mean much

(Facing page.) Wilt Chamberlain, one of the all-time great players, set many picks for me during the 1971-72 Laker championship season.

more to me than any individual achievements. Even though I take a great deal of pride in my ability to score, I would rather score fewer points and win than score more and lose. Once you have ended a season with a championship, you can rest knowing you have done all you can.

When I leave the game, I will look back on my career with pride and satisfaction. I have reaped many rewards from basketball, there is no question about that. But all of it has just come my way as a by-product of the sport I love.

index

140